Truth Serum

Truth Serum

~~~~~~~~~~~~~~~~~~ m e m o i r s

Bernard Cooper

Houghton Mifflin Company · Boston · New York
1996

For information about permission to reproduce selections from this book,
write to Permissions, Houghton Mifflin Company, 215 Park Avenue South,
New York, New York 10003.

For information about this and other Houghton Mifflin trade and reference
books and multimedia products, visit The Bookstore at Houghton Mifflin
on the World Wide Web at http://www.hmco.com/trade/.

Library of Congress Cataloging-in-Publication Data
Cooper, Bernard, date.
  Truth serum : memoirs / Bernard Cooper.
    p.   cm.
  ISBN 0-395-74539-X
    1. Cooper, Bernard, 1951–   — Biography. 2. Authors, American
— 20th century — Biography. 3. Gay men — United States —
Biography.   I. Title.
PS3553.057982463   1996   95-38984
813'.54 — dc20   CIP   [B]

Printed in the United States of America

QUM 10 9 8 7 6 5 4 3 2 1

Book design by Melodie Wertelet

Some of the memoirs in this collection have appeared elsewhere, in slightly different
form: "101 Ways to Cook Hamburger" in *Harper's Magazine;* "Burl's" in *The Los Angeles
Times Magazine* and *The Best American Essays 1995,* edited by Jamaica Kincaid; "Imitation
of Life" in *The San Diego Reader;* "Arson" in *His: Brilliant New Fiction by Gay Writers;*
"Truth Serum" in *Harper's Magazine, The 1995 O. Henry Prize Collection,* and *Brother and
Sister: Gay Men and Lesbians Write about Each Other;* "The Fine Art of Sighing" in *The
Paris Review;* "Picking Plums" in *Harper's Magazine, A Member of the Family: Gay Men
Write about Their Families, Turning Toward Home: Reflections on the Family from Harper's
Magazine,* and *The Oxford Book of Aging;* "Train of Thought" in *The Gettysburg Review*
and *Harper's Magazine;* and "Tone Poem" in *The Paris Review.*

For Brian

~~~~~~~~~~~~~~~~~~

The author wishes to thank the following people
for their kindness, advice, and forbearance:

Steven Barclay, Steve Blakley, Clifford Chase,
John Chase, Robert Dawidoff, Jacqueline De An-
gelis, Amy Gerstler, Sloan Harris, Amy Hempel,
Richard Howard, Terryl Hunter, David Leavitt,
Rondo Mieczkowski, Judith Moore, Linda Norlen,
Gordon Pollack, Kit Rachlis, Greg Riley, Aleida
Rodríguez, Dawn Seferian, Ilena Silverman, and
Benjamin Weissman.

And especially Jill Climent, Jeff Hammond,
Michelle Huneven, Tom Knechtel, and Bia Lowe.

Contents

". . . but there it was, I knew it to be true,
and if it was impossible then the definition
of possibility was inadequate."

～ Jan Morris

Truth Serum

Where to Begin

~~~~~~~~~~~~~~~~~~~~~~~~~

One day I was looking through an issue of *Art in America* when I came across a reproduction of the most complicated painting I'd ever seen. Rendered in bright colors and with painstaking precision, the canvas contained, among a hundred other images, a naked man and woman, a passenger jet, a bouquet of red roses, a five-dollar bill, a wristwatch, a pencil, and a slab of raw steak. Nowhere did sky or sunlight squeak through. There was, in fact, no foreground or background, none of the comforts of scale or perspective. Each thing seemed to be tossed on a heap, jostling for space and attention. The other paintings in the magazine — minimal this and abstract that — looked arid and bland by comparison, as uneventful as a Sunday in the suburbs. As I brought the page closer, astonished by the craftsmanship, a cocker spaniel or a telephone suddenly emerged from the chaos.

I couldn't help but think that it would have taken someone many, many years to complete such a painting. It's even possible that the artist, a man I'd never heard of before or since, invented a few mechanical aids to help him with his mission: a splint to hold up his cramping hand, flashlights affixed to his thick prescription glasses. Or he might have gone blind and mad in the process, like someone condemned to spend his life embroidering a circus tent.

Beneath the reproduction it read, "*A Grain of Sand,* 1969. Acrylic on canvas (detail)." Wow, I thought, if that's a detail, imagine the whole painting. And if the whole painting is a single grain of sand, imagine the beach, the coastline, the continent rimmed by a trillion grains.

This painting comes to mind whenever I try to write about my life. Sure, such and such happened. But what about that and that and that, till the picture is jammed to overflowing, and I don't know where to begin.

I can still see the nurse — Sister Mary Something-or-other — coming though the door. Her pale face peers out from her habit. She regards me in my mother's arms, tells me I'm tiny, then turns and walks away. Correct me if I'm wrong, but the maternity ward was on the seventh floor of Queen of Angels Hospital and my mother's room, facing south, overlooked the Hollywood Freeway, which wasn't nearly as crowded then as it is today. I remember the swoosh of afternoon traffic wafting through the open window. Mother's hospital gown was strewn with blue dots, her eyes as bright as milk.

Which reminds me of when I twinkled in my father's eye. I was nothing back then but a yen for affection, a shimmer of expectancy as he pulled my future mother to the sheets. Her wavy hair splashed upon the pillow. As he undid the buttons of her sleeveless blouse, he also managed to tug off his tie and toss it over his shoulder. His zeal caused my mother to grab him and laugh. His last thought before he was too glad to think: *I wish I had more hands.*

But let's go back further to the static of nonbeing, so like a sandstorm. Every infinitesimal grain contained a vague potential charge, a quasi-almost-stab-at-something, a not-quite-manifest-inkling-of-matter. The air around me felt quiet but alive, like the pause before a clap of thunder. The idea dawned that I might take shape, might take my place among abundance. Life was so much fresher then, my molecules as wet as drops of paint, my soon-to-be memories too numerous to mention.

101 Ways
to Cook
Hamburger

Theresa Sanchez sat behind me in ninth-grade algebra. When Mr. Hubbley faced the blackboard, I'd turn around to see what she was reading; each week a new book was wedged inside her copy of *Today's Equations*. The deception worked; from Mr. Hubbley's point of view, Theresa was engrossed in the value of X, but I knew otherwise. One week she perused *The Wisdom of the Orient*, and I could tell from Theresa's contemplative expression that the book contained exotic thoughts, guidelines handed down from on high. Another week it was a paperback novel whose title, *Let Me Live My Life*, appeared in bold print atop every page, and whose cover, a gauzy photograph of a woman biting a strand of pearls, her head thrown back in ecstasy, confirmed my suspicion that Theresa Sanchez was mature beyond her years. She was the tallest girl in school. Her bouffant hairdo, streaked with blond, was higher than the flaccid bouffants of other girls. Her smooth skin, plucked eyebrows, and painted fingernails suggested hours of pampering, a worldly and sensual vanity that placed her within the domain of adults. Smiling dimly, steeped in daydreams, Theresa moved through the crowded halls with a languid, self-satisfied indifference to those around her. "You are merely children," her posture seemed to say, "I can't be bothered." The week Theresa hid *101 Ways to Cook Hamburger* behind her algebra book, I could stand it no longer, and after the bell rang, ventured a question.

"Because I'm having a dinner party," said Theresa. "Just a couple of intimate friends."

No fourteen-year-old I knew had ever given a dinner party, let alone used the word "intimate" in conversation. "Don't you have a mother?" I asked.

Theresa sighed a weary sigh, suffered my strange inquiry. "Don't be so naive," she said. "Everyone has a mother." She waved her hand to indicate the brick school buildings outside the window. "A higher education should have taught you that." Theresa draped an angora sweater over her shoulders, scooped her books from the graffiti-covered desk, and just as she was about to walk away, turned and asked me, "Are you a fag?"

There wasn't the slightest hint of rancor or condescension in her voice. The tone was direct, casual. Still I was stunned, giving a sidelong glance to make sure no one had heard. "No," I said. Blurted really, with too much defensiveness, too much transparent fear in my response. Octaves lower than usual, I tried a "Why?"

Theresa shrugged. "Oh, I don't know. I have lots of friends who are fags. You remind me of them." Seeing me bristle, Theresa added, "It was just a guess." I watched her erect angora back as she sauntered out the classroom door.

She had made an incisive and timely guess. Only days before, I'd invited Grady Rogers to my house after school to go swimming. The instant Grady shot from the pool, shaking water from his orange hair, his freckled shoulders shining, my attraction to members of my own sex became a matter I could no longer suppress or rationalize. Sturdy and boisterous and gap-toothed, Grady was an inveterate back slapper, a formidable arm wrestler, a wizard at basketball. Grady was a boy at home in his body.

My body was a marvel I hadn't gotten used to; my arms and legs would sometimes act of their own accord, knocking over a glass at dinner or flinching at an oncoming pitch. I was never singled out as a sissy, but I could have been just as easily as Bobby Keagan, a gentle, intelligent, and introverted boy reviled by my classmates. And although I had always been aware of a tacit rapport with Bobby, a suspicion that I might find with him a rich friendship, I stayed away. Instead, I emulated Grady in the belief that being seen with him, being like him, would somehow vanquish my self-doubt, would make me normal by association.

Apart from his athletic prowess, Grady had been gifted with all the trappings of what I imagined to be a charmed life: a fastidious, aproned mother who radiated calm and maternal concern, a ruddy, stoic father with a knack for home repairs. Even the Rogerses' small suburban house in Hollywood, with its spindly Colonial furniture and chintz curtains, was a testament to normalcy.

Grady and his family bore little resemblance to my clan of Eastern European Jews, a dark and vociferous people who ate with abandon — matzo and halvah and gefilte fish; foods the goyim couldn't pronounce — who cajoled one another during endless games of canasta, making the simplest remark about the weather into a lengthy philosophical discourse on the sun and the seasons and the passage of time. My mother was a chain smoker, a dervish in a frowsy housedress. She showed her love in the most peculiar and obsessive ways, like spending hours extracting every seed from a watermelon before she served it in perfectly bite-sized geometric pieces. Preoccupied and perpetually frantic, my mother succumbed to bouts of absentmindedness so profound she'd forget what she was saying in midsentence, smile and blush and walk away. A divorce attorney, my father wore roomy, iridescent suits, and the intricacies, the deceits inherent in his profession, had the effect of making him forever tense and vigilant. He was "all wound up," as my mother put it. But when he relaxed, his laughter was explosive, his disposition prankish: "Walk this way," a waitress would say, leading us to our table, and my father would mimic the way she walked, arms akimbo, hips liquid, while my mother and I were wracked with laughter. Buoyant or brooding, my parents' moods were unpredictable, and in a household fraught with extravagant emotion it was odd and awful to keep my longing secret.

One day I made the mistake of asking my mother what a fag was. I knew exactly what Theresa had meant, but hoped against hope it was not what I thought; maybe *fag* was some French word, a harmless term like *naive*. My mother turned from the stove, flew at me, and grabbed me by the shoulders. "Did someone call you that?" she cried.

"Not me," I said. "Bobby Keagan."

"Oh," she said, loosening her grip. She was visibly relieved. And didn't answer. The answer was unthinkable.

*

For weeks after, I shook with the reverberations from that afternoon in the kitchen with my mother, pained by the memory of her shocked expression and, most of all, her silence. My longing was wrong in the eyes of my mother, whose hazel eyes were the eyes of the world, and if that longing continued unchecked, the unwieldy shape of my fate would be cast, and I'd be subjected to a lifetime of scorn.

During the remainder of the semester, I became the scientist of my own desire, plotting ways to change my yearning for boys into a yearning for girls. I had enough evidence to believe that any habit, regardless of how compulsive, how deeply ingrained, could be broken once and for all: the plastic cigarette my mother purchased at the Thrifty pharmacy (one end was red to approximate an ember, the other tan like a filter tip) was designed to wean her from the real thing. To change a behavior required self-analysis, cold resolve, and the substitution of one thing for another: plastic, say, for tobacco. Could I also find a substitute for

Grady? What I needed to do, I figured, was kiss a girl and learn to like it.

This conclusion was affirmed one Sunday morning when my father, seeing me wrinkle my nose at the pink slabs of lox he layered on a bagel, tried to convince me of its salty appeal. "You should try some," he said. "You don't know what you're missing."

"It's loaded with protein," added my mother, slapping a platter of sliced onions onto the dinette table. She hovered above us, cinching up her housedress, eyes wet from onion fumes, a mock cigarette dangling from her lips.

My father sat there chomping with gusto, emitting a couple of hearty grunts to dramatize his satisfaction. And still I was not convinced. After a loud and labored swallow, he told me I may not be fond of lox today, but sooner or later I'd learn to like it. One's tastes, he assured me, are destined to change.

"Live," shouted my mother over the rumble of the Mixmaster. "Expand your horizons. Try new things." And the room grew fragrant with the batter of a spice cake.

The opportunity to put their advice into practice, and try out my plan to adapt to girls, came the following week when Debbie Coburn, a member of Mr. Hubbley's algebra class, invited me to a party. She cornered me in the hall, furtive as a spy, telling me her parents would be gone for the evening and slipping into my palm a wrinkled sheet of notebook paper. On it were her address and telephone number, the lavender ink in a tidy cursive. "Wear cologne," she advised, wary eyes darting back and forth. "It's a make-out party. Anything can happen."

The Santa Ana winds blew relentlessly the night of Debbie's party, careening down the slopes of the Hollywood Hills, shaking the road signs and stoplights in its path. As I walked down Beachwood Avenue, trees thrashed, surrendered their leaves, and carob pods bombarded the pavement. The sky was a deep but luminous blue, the air hot, abrasive, electric. I had to squint in order to check the number of the Coburns' apartment, a three-story building with glitter embedded in its stucco walls. Above the honeycombed balconies was a sign that read *Beachwood Terrace* in lavender script resembling Debbie's.

From down the hall, I could hear the plaintive strains of Little Anthony's "Goin' Out of My Head." Debbie answered the door bedecked in an empire dress, the bodice blue with orange polka dots, the rest a sheath of black and white stripes. "Op art," proclaimed Debbie. She turned in a circle, then proudly announced that she'd rolled her hair in frozen orange juice cans. She patted the huge unmoving curls and dragged me inside. Reflections from the swimming pool in the courtyard, its surface ruffled by wind, shuddered over the ceiling and walls. A dozen of my classmates were seated on the sofa or huddled together in corners, their whispers full of excited imminence, their bodies barely discernible in the dim light. Drapes flanking the sliding glass doors bowed out with every gust of wind, and it seemed that the room might lurch from its foundations and sail with its cargo of silhouettes into the hot October night.

Grady was the last to arrive. He tossed a six-pack of beer into Debbie's arms, barreled toward me, and slapped my back. His hair was slicked back with Vitalis, lacquered furrows left by the comb. The wind hadn't shifted a single hair. "Ya ready?" he asked, flashing the gap between his front teeth and leering into the darkened room. "You bet," I lied.

Once the beers had been passed around, Debbie provoked everyone's attention by flicking on the overhead light. "OK," she called. "Find a partner." This was the blunt command of a hostess determined to have her guests aroused in an orderly fashion. Everyone blinked, shuffled about, and grabbed a member of the opposite sex. Sheila Garabedian landed beside me (entirely at random, though I wanted to believe she was driven by passion), her timid smile giving way to plain fear as the light went out.

Nothing for a moment but the heave of the wind and the distant banter of dogs. I caught a whiff of Sheila's perfume, as tangy and sweet as Hawaiian Punch. I probed her face with my own, grazing the small scallop of an ear, a velvety temple, and though Sheila's trembling made me want to stop, I persisted with my mission until I found her lips, as tightly sealed as a private letter. I held my mouth over hers and gathered her shoulders closer, resigned to the possibility that, no matter how long we stood there, Sheila was too scared to kiss me back. Still, she exhaled through her nose, and I listened to the squeak of every breath as though it were a sigh of inordinate pleasure. Diving within myself, I monitored my heartbeat and respiration, trying to will stimulation into being, and all the while an image intruded, an image of Grady erupting from our pool, rivulets of water sliding down his chest. "Change," shouted Debbie, switching on the light. Sheila thanked me, pulled away, and continued her routine of gracious terror with every boy throughout the room. It didn't matter whom I held — Margaret Sims, Betty Vernon, Elizabeth Lee — my experiment was a failure; I continued to picture Grady's wet chest, and Debbie would bellow "Change!" with such fervor, it could have been my own voice, my own incessant reprimand.

Our hostess commandeered the light switch for nearly half an hour. Whenever the light came on, I watched Grady pivot his head toward the newest prospect, his eyebrows arched in expectation, his neck blooming with hickeys, his hair, at last, in disarray. All that shuffling across the carpet charged everyone's arms and lips with static, and eventually, between low moans and soft osculations, I could hear the clack of tiny sparks and see them flare here and there in the dark like meager, short-lived stars.

*

I saw Theresa, as sultry and aloof as ever, read three more books — *North American Reptiles, Bonjour Tristesse,* and *MGM: A Pictorial History* — before she vanished early in December. Rumors of her fate abounded. Debbie Coburn swore that Theresa had been "knocked up" by an older man, a traffic cop, she thought, or a grocer. Nearly quivering with relish, Debbie told Grady and me about the home for unwed mothers in the San Fernando Valley, a compound teeming with pregnant girls who had nothing to do but touch their stomachs and contemplate their mistake. Even Bobby Keagan, who took Theresa's place behind me in algebra, had a theory regarding her disappearance colored by his own wish for escape; he imagined that Theresa, disillusioned with society, booked passage to a tropical island, there to live out the rest of her days without restrictions or ridicule. "No wonder she flunked out of school," I overheard Mr. Hubbley tell a fellow teacher one afternoon. "Her head was always in a book."

Along with Theresa went my secret, or at least the dread that she might divulge it, and I felt, for a while, exempt from suspicion. I was, however, to run across Theresa one last time. It happened during a period of torrential rain that, according to reports on the six o'clock news, washed houses from the hillsides and flooded the downtown streets. The halls of Joseph Le Conte Junior High were festooned with Christmas decorations: crepe-paper garlands, wreaths studded with plastic berries, and one requisite Star of David twirling above the attendance desk. In arts and crafts, our teacher, Gerald (he was the only teacher who allowed us, *required* us, to call him by his first name), handed out blocks of balsa wood and instructed us to carve them into bugs. We would paint eyes and antennae with tempera and hang them on a Christmas tree he'd made the previous night. "*Voilà,*" he crooned, unveiling his creation from a burlap sack. Before us sat a tortured scrub, a wardrobe's worth of wire hangers that were bent like branches and soldered together. Gerald credited

his inspiration to a Charles Addams cartoon he'd seen in which
Morticia, grimly preparing for the holidays, hangs vampire bats
on a withered pine. "All that red and green," said Gerald. "So
predictable. So boring."

As I chiseled a beetle and listened to rain pummel the earth,
Gerald handed me an envelope and asked me to take it to Mr.
Kendrick, the drama teacher. I would have thought nothing of
his request if I hadn't seen Theresa on my way down the hall. She
was cleaning out her locker, blithely dropping the sum of its
contents — pens and textbooks and mimeographs — into a trash
can. "Have a nice life," she sang as I passed. I mustered the
courage to ask her what had happened. We stood alone in the
silent hall, the reflections of wreaths and garlands submerged in
brown linoleum.

"I transferred to another school. They don't have grades or
bells and you get to study whatever you want." Theresa was
quick to sense my incredulity. "Honest," she said. "The school is
progressive." She gazed into a glass cabinet that held the trophies
of track meets and intramural spelling bees. "God," she said with
a sigh, "this place is so . . . barbaric." I was still trying to decide
whether to believe her story when she asked me where I was
headed. "Dear," she said, her exclamation pooling in the silence,
"that's no ordinary note, if you catch my drift." The envelope
was blank and white; I looked up at Theresa, baffled. "Don't be
so naive," she muttered, tossing an empty bottle of nail polish
into the trash can. It struck bottom with a resolute thud. "Well,"
she said, closing her locker and breathing deeply, "bon voyage."
Theresa swept through the double doors and in seconds her
figure was obscured by rain.

As I walked toward Mr. Kendrick's room, I could feel Theresa's insinuation burrow in. I stood for a moment and watched
Mr. Kendrick through the pane in the door. He paced intently in
front of the class, handsome in his shirt and tie, reading from a

thick book. Chalked on the blackboard behind him was THE
ODYSSEY BY HOMER. I have no recollection of how Mr. Kendrick reacted to the note, whether he accepted it with pleasure or
embarrassment, slipped it into his desk drawer or the pocket of
his shirt. I have scavenged that day in retrospect, trying to see
Mr. Kendrick's expression, wondering if he acknowledged me in
any way as his liaison. All I recall is the sight of his mime through
a pane of glass, a lone man mouthing an epic, his gestures ardent
in empty air.

Had I delivered a declaration of love? I was haunted by the
need to know. In fantasy, a kettle shot steam, the glue released its
grip, and I read the letter with impunity. But how would such a
letter begin? Did the common endearments apply? This was a
message between two men, a message for which I had no precedent, and when I tried to envision the contents, apart from a
hasty, impassioned scrawl, my imagination faltered.

Once or twice I witnessed Gerald and Mr. Kendrick walk
together into the faculty lounge or say hello at the water fountain, but there was nothing especially clandestine or flirtatious in
their manner. Besides, no matter how acute my scrutiny, I wasn't
sure, short of a kiss, exactly what to look for — what semaphore
of gesture, what encoded word; I suspected there were signs,
covert signs that would give them away, just as I'd unwittingly
given myself away to Theresa.

In the school library, a *Webster's* unabridged dictionary lay on
a wooden podium, and I padded toward it with apprehension;
along with clues to the bond between my teachers, I risked discovering information that might incriminate me as well. I had
decided to consult the dictionary during lunch period when most
of the students would be on the playground. I clutched my notebook, moving in such a way as to appear both studious and nonchalant, actually believing that, unless I took precautions, someone would see me and guess what I was up to. The closer I came

to the podium, the more obvious, I thought, was my endeavor; I felt like the model of the Visible Man in our science class, my heart's undulations, my overwrought nerves, legible through transparent skin. A couple of kids riffled through the card catalogue. The librarian, a skinny woman whose perpetual whisper and rubber-soled shoes caused her to drift through the room like a phantom, didn't seem to register my presence. Though I'd looked up dozens of words before, the pages felt strange beneath my fingers. *Homer* was the first word I saw. *Hominid. Homogenize.* I feigned interest and skirted other words before I found the word I was after. Following the boldfaced ho•mo•sex•u•al was this terse definition: *adj. Pertaining to, characteristic of, or exhibiting homosexuality. — n. A homosexual person.* I read the definition again and again, hoping the words would yield more than they could. I shut the dictionary, swallowed hard, and, none the wiser, hurried away.

As for Gerald and Mr. Kendrick, I never discovered evidence to prove or dispute Theresa's claim. By the following summer, however, I had overheard from my peers a confounding amount about homosexuals: they wore green on Thursday, couldn't whistle, hypnotized boys with a piercing glance. To this lore, Grady added a surefire test to ferret them out.

"A test?" I said.

"You ask a guy to look at his fingernails, and if he looks at them like this" — Grady closed his fingers into a fist and examined his nails with manly detachment — "then he's OK. But if he does this" — he held out his hands at arm's length, splayed his fingers, and coyly cocked his head — "you'd better watch out." Once he'd completed his demonstration, Grady peeled off his shirt and plunged into our pool. I dove in after him. It was early June, the sky immense, glassy, placid. My father was cooking spareribs on the barbecue, an artist with a basting brush. His apron bore the caricature of a frazzled French chef. Mother curled on a chaise longue, plumes of smoke wafting from her nostrils. In a stupor of contentment she took another drag, closed her eyes, and arched her face toward the sun.

Grady dog-paddled through the deep end, spouting a fountain of chlorinated water. Despite shame and confusion, my longing for him hadn't diminished; it continued to thrive without air and light, like a luminous fish in the dregs of the sea. In the name of play, I swam up behind him, encircled his shoulders, astonished by his taut flesh. The two of us flailed, pretended to drown. Beneath the heavy press of water, Grady's orange hair wavered, a flame that couldn't be doused.

*

I've lived with a man for eleven years. Some nights, when I'm half asleep and the room is suffused with blue light, I reach out to touch the expanse of his back, and it seems as if my fingers sink into his skin, and I feel the pleasure a diver feels the instant he enters a body of water.

I have few regrets. But one is that I didn't say to Theresa, "Of course I'm a fag." Maybe I'd have met her friends. Or become friends with her. Imagine the meals we might have concocted: hamburger Stroganoff, Swedish meatballs in a sweet translucent sauce, steaming slabs of Salisbury steak.

Burl's

~~~~~~~~~~

I loved the restaurant's name, a compact curve of a word. Its sign, five big letters rimmed in neon, hovered above the roof. I almost never saw the sign with its neon lit; my parents took me there for early summer dinners, and even by the time we left — Father cleaning his teeth with a toothpick, Mother carrying steak bones in a doggie bag — the sky was still bright. Heat rippled off the cars parked along Hollywood Boulevard, the asphalt gummy from hours of sun.

With its sleek architecture, chrome appliances, and arctic temperature, Burl's offered a refuge from the street. We usually sat at one of the booths in front of the plate glass windows. During our dinner, people came to a halt before the news-vending machine on the corner and burrowed in their pockets and purses for change.

The waitresses at Burl's wore brown uniforms edged in checked gingham. From their breast pockets frothed white lace handkerchiefs. In between reconnaissance missions to the tables, they busied themselves behind the counter and shouted "Tuna to travel" or "Scorch that patty" to a harried short-order cook who manned the grill. Miniature pitchers of cream and individual pats of butter were extracted from an industrial refrigerator. Coca-Cola shot from a glinting spigot. Waitresses dodged and bumped one another, as frantic as atoms.

My parents usually lingered after the meal, nursing cups of

coffee while I played with the beads of condensation on my glass of ice water, tasted Tabasco sauce, or twisted pieces of my paper napkin into mangled animals. One evening, annoyed with my restlessness, my father gave me a dime and asked me to buy him a *Herald Examiner* from the vending machine in front of the restaurant.

Shouldering open the heavy glass door, I was seared by a sudden gust of heat. Traffic roared past me and stirred the air. Walking toward the newspaper machine, I held the dime so tightly, it seemed to melt in my palm. Duty made me feel large and important. I inserted the dime and opened the box, yanking a *Herald* from the spring contraption that held it as tight as a mousetrap. When I turned around, paper in hand, I saw two women walking toward me.

Their high heels clicked on the sun-baked pavement. They were tall, broad-shouldered women who moved with a mixture of haste and defiance. They'd teased their hair into nearly identical black beehives. Dangling earrings flashed in the sun, as brilliant as prisms. Each of them wore the kind of clinging, strapless outfit my mother referred to as a cocktail dress. The silky fabric — one dress was purple, the other pink — accentuated their breasts and hips and rippled with insolent highlights. The dresses exposed their bare arms, the slope of their shoulders, and the smooth, powdered plane of flesh where their cleavage began.

I owned at the time a book called *Things for Boys and Girls to Do*. There were pages to color, intricate mazes, and connect-the-dots. But another type of puzzle came to mind as I watched those women walking toward me: What's Wrong with This Picture? Say the drawing of a dining room looked normal at first glance; on closer inspection, a chair was missing its leg and the man who sat atop it wore half a pair of glasses.

The women had Adam's apples.

The closer they came, the shallower my breathing. I blocked

the sidewalk, an incredulous child stalled in their path. When they saw me staring, they shifted their purses and linked their arms. There was something sisterly and conspiratorial about their sudden closeness. Though their mouths didn't open, I thought they might have been communicating without moving their lips, so telepathic did they seem as they joined arms and pressed together, synchronizing their heavy steps. The pages of the *Herald* fluttered in the wind; I felt them against my arm, as light as batted lashes.

The woman in pink shot me a haughty glance, and yet she seemed pleased that I'd taken notice, hungry to be admired by a man, or even an awestruck eight-year-old boy. She tried to stifle a grin, her red lipstick more voluptuous than the lips it painted. Rouge deepened her cheekbones. Eye shadow dusted her lids, a clumsy abundance of blue. Her face was like a page in *Things for Boys and Girls to Do*, colored by a kid who went outside the lines.

At close range, I saw that her wig was slightly askew. I was certain it was a wig because my mother owned several; three Styrofoam heads lined a shelf in my mother's closet; upon them were perched a pageboy, an empress, and a baby doll, all in shades of auburn. The woman in the pink dress wore her wig like a crown of glory.

But it was the woman in the purple dress who passed nearest me, and I saw that her jaw was heavily powdered, a half-successful attempt to disguise the telltale shadow of a beard. Just as I noticed this, her heel caught on a crack in the pavement and she reeled on her stilettos. It was then that I witnessed a rift in her composure, a window through which I could glimpse the shades of maleness that her dress and wig and make-up obscured. She shifted her shoulders and threw out her hands like a surfer riding a curl. The instant she regained her balance, she smoothed her dress, patted her hair, and sauntered onward.

Any woman might be a man; the fact of it clanged through the chambers of my brain. In broad day, in the midst of traffic, with my parents drinking coffee a few feet away, I felt as if everything I understood, everything I had taken for granted up to that moment — the curve of the earth, the heat of the sun, the reliability of my own eyes — had been squeezed out of me. Who were those men? Did they help each other get inside those dresses? How many other people and things were not what they seemed? From the back, the imposters looked like women once again, slinky and curvaceous, purple and pink. I watched them disappear into the distance, their disguises so convincing that other people on the street seemed to take no notice, and for a moment I wondered if I had imagined the whole encounter, a visitation by two unlikely muses.

Frozen in the middle of the sidewalk, I caught my reflection in the window of Burl's, a silhouette floating between his parents. They faced one another across a table. Once the solid embodiments of woman and man, pedestrians and traffic appeared to pass through them.

*

There were some mornings, seconds before my eyes opened and my senses gathered into consciousness, that the child I was seemed to hover above the bed, and I couldn't tell what form my waking would take — the body of a boy or the body of a girl. Finally stirring, I'd blink against the early light and greet each incarnation as a male with mild surprise. My sex, in other words, didn't seem to be an absolute fact so much as a pleasant, recurring accident.

By the age of eight, I'd experienced this groggy phenomenon several times. Those ethereal moments above my bed made waking up in the tangled blankets, a boy steeped in body heat, all the more astonishing. That this might be an unusual experience never occurred to me; it was one among a flood of sensations I could neither name nor ignore.

And so, shocked as I was when those transvestites passed me in front of Burl's, they confirmed something about which I already had an inkling: the hazy border between the sexes. My father, after all, raised his pinky when he drank from a teacup, and my mother looked as faded and plain as my father until she fixed her hair and painted her face.

Like most children, I once thought it possible to divide the world into male and female columns. Blue/Pink. Roosters/Hens. Trousers/Skirts. Such divisions were easy, not to mention comforting, for they simplified matter into compatible pairs. But there also existed a vast range of things that didn't fit neatly into either camp: clocks, milk, telephones, grass. There were nights I fell into a fitful sleep while trying to sex the world correctly.

Nothing typified the realms of male and female as clearly as my parents' walk-in closets. Home alone for any length of time, I always found my way inside them. I could stare at my parents' clothes for hours, grateful for the stillness and silence, haunting the very heart of their privacy.

The overhead light in my father's closet was a bare bulb. Whenever I groped for the chain in the dark, it wagged back and forth and resisted my grasp. Once the light clicked on, I saw dozens of ties hanging like stalactites. A monogrammed silk bathrobe sagged from a hook, a gift my father had received on a long-ago birthday and, thinking it fussy, rarely wore. Shirts were cramped together along the length of an aluminum pole, their starched sleeves sticking out as if in a halfhearted gesture of greeting. The medicinal odor of mothballs permeated the boxer shorts that were folded and stacked in a built-in drawer. Immaculate underwear was proof of a tenderness my mother couldn't otherwise express; she may not have touched my father often, but she laundered his boxers with infinite care. Even back then, I suspected that a sense of duty was the final erotic link between them.

Sitting in a neat row on the closet floor were my father's boots and slippers and dress shoes. I'd try on his wing tips and clomp around, slipping out of them with every step. My wary, unnatural stride made me all the more desperate to effect some authority. I'd whisper orders to imagined lackeys and take my invisible wife in my arms. But no matter how much I wanted them to fit, those shoes were as cold and hard as marble.

My mother's shoes were just as uncomfortable, but a lot more fun. From a brightly colored array of pumps and sling-backs, I'd pick a pair with the glee and deliberation of someone choosing a chocolate. Whatever embarrassment I felt was overwhelmed by the exhilaration of being taller in a pair of high heels. Things will look like this someday, I said to myself, gazing out from my new and improved vantage point as if from a crow's nest. Calves elongated, hands on my hips, I gauged each step so I didn't fall over and moved with what might have passed for grace had someone seen me, a possibility I scrupulously avoided by locking the door.

Back and forth I went. The longer I wore a pair of heels, the better my balance. In the periphery of my vision, the shelf of wigs looked like a throng of kindly bystanders. Light streamed down from a high window, causing crystal bottles to glitter, the air ripe with perfume. A make-up mirror above the dressing table invited my self-absorption. Sound was muffled. Time slowed. It seemed as if nothing bad could happen as long as I stayed within those walls.

Though I'd never been discovered in my mother's closet, my parents knew that I was drawn toward girlish things — dolls and jump rope and jewelry — as well as to the games and preoccupations that were expected of a boy. I'm not sure now if it was my effeminacy itself that bothered them so much as my ability to slide back and forth, without the slightest warning, between male and female mannerisms. After I'd finished building the model of an F-17 bomber, say, I'd sit back to examine my handiwork, pursing my lips in concentration and crossing my legs at the knee.

One day my mother caught me standing in the middle of my bedroom doing an imitation of Mary Injijikian, a dark, over-eager Armenian girl with whom I believed myself to be in love, not only because she was pretty, but because I wanted to be like her. Collector of effortless A's, Mary seemed to know all the answers in class. Before the teacher had even finished asking a question, Mary would let out a little grunt and practically levi-tate out of her seat, as if her hand were filled with helium. "Could we please hear from someone else today besides Miss Injijikian," the teacher would say. *Miss Injijikian*. Those were the words I was repeating over and over to myself when my mother caught me. To utter them was rhythmic, delicious, and under their spell I raised my hand and wiggled like Mary. I heard a cough and spun around. My mother froze in the doorway. She clutched the folded sheets to her stomach and turned without saying a word. My sudden flush of shame confused me. Weren't boys supposed to swoon over girls? Hadn't I seen babbling, heartsick men in a dozen movies?

Shortly after the Injijikian incident, my parents decided to send me to gymnastics class at the Downtown Athletic Club, a brick relic of a building on Grand Avenue. One of the oldest establishments of its kind in Los Angeles, the club prohibited women from the premises. My parents didn't have to say it aloud: they hoped a fraternal atmosphere would toughen me up and tilt me toward the male side of my nature.

My father drove me downtown so I could sign up for the class, meet the instructor, and get a tour of the place. On the way there, he reminisced about sports. Since he'd grown up in a rough

Philadelphia neighborhood, sports consisted of kick-the-can, or rolling a hoop down the street with a stick. The more he talked about his physical prowess, the more convinced I became that my daydreams and shyness were a disappointment to him.

The hushed lobby of the Athletic Club was paneled in dark wood. A few solitary figures were hidden in wing chairs. My father and I introduced ourselves to a man at the front desk who seemed unimpressed by our presence. His aloofness unnerved me, which wasn't hard considering that no matter how my parents put it, I knew that sending me here was a form of disapproval, a way of banishing the part of me they didn't care to know.

A call went out over the intercom for someone to show us around. While we waited, I noticed that the sand in the standing ashtrays had been raked into perfect furrows. The glossy leaves of the potted plants looked as if they'd been polished by hand. The place seemed more like a well-tended hotel than an athletic club. Finally, a stoop-shouldered old man hobbled toward us, his head shrouded in a cloud of white hair. He wore a T-shirt that said INSTRUCTOR, but his arms were so wrinkled and anemic, I thought I might have misread it. While we followed him to the elevator — it would be easier, he said, than taking the stairs — I readjusted my expectations, which had involved fantasies of a hulking drill sergeant barking orders at a flock of scrawny boys.

We got off the elevator on the second floor. The instructor, mumbling to himself and never turning around to see if we were behind him, showed us where the gymnastics class took place. I'm certain the building was big, but the size of the room must be exaggerated by a trick of memory, because when I envision it, I picture a vast and windowless warehouse. Mats covered the wooden floor. Here and there, in remote and lonely pools of light, stood a pommel horse, a balance beam, and parallel bars.

Tiers of bleachers rose into darkness. Unlike the cloistered air of a closet, the room seemed incomplete without a crowd.

Next we visited the dressing room, empty except for a naked, middle-aged man. He sat on a narrow bench and clipped his formidable toenails. Moles dotted his back. He glistened like a fish.

We continued to follow the instructor down an aisle lined with numbered lockers. At the far end, steam billowed from the doorway that led to the showers. Fresh towels stacked on a nearby table made me think of my mother; I knew she liked to have me at home with her — I was often her only companion — and I resented her complicity in the plan to send me here.

The tour ended when the instructor gave me a sign-up sheet. Only a few names preceded mine. They were signatures, or so I imagined, of other soft and wayward sons.

When the day of the first gymnastics class arrived, my mother gave me money and a gym bag (along with a clean towel, she'd packed a banana and a napkin) and sent me to the corner of Hollywood and Western to wait for a bus. The sun was bright, the traffic heavy. While I sat there, an argument raged inside my head, the familiar, battering debate between the wish to be like other boys and the wish to be like myself. Why shouldn't I simply get up and go back home, where I'd be left alone to read and think? On the other hand, wouldn't life be easier if I liked athletics, or learned to like them? No sooner did I steel my resolve to get on the bus, than I thought of something better: I could spend the morning wandering through Woolworth's, then tell my parents I'd gone to the class. But would my lie stand up to scrutiny? As I practiced describing phantom gymnastics — *And then we did cartwheels and, boy, was I dizzy* — I became aware of a car circling the block. It was a large car in whose shaded interior I could barely make out the driver, but I thought it might be the man who owned the local pet store. I'd often gone there on the pretext of looking at the cocker spaniel puppies huddled together in their pen, but I really went to gawk at the owner, whose tan chest, in the V of his shirt, was the place I most wanted to rest my head. Every time the man moved, counting stock or writing a receipt, his shirt parted, my mouth went dry, and I smelled the musk of sawdust and dogs.

I found myself hoping that the driver was the man who ran the pet store. I was thrilled by the unlikely possibility that the sight of me, slumped on a bus bench in my T-shirt and shorts, had caused such a man to circle the block. Up to that point in my life, lovemaking hovered somewhere in the future, an impulse a boy might aspire to but didn't indulge. And there I was, sitting on a bus bench in the middle of the city, dreaming I could seduce an adult; I showered the owner of the pet store with kisses and, as aquariums bubbled, birds sang, and mice raced in a wire wheel, slipped my hand beneath his shirt. The roar of traffic brought me to my senses. I breathed deeply and blinked against the sun. I crossed my legs at the knee in order to hide an erection. My fantasy left me both drained and changed. The continent of sex had drifted closer.

The car made another round. This time the driver leaned across the passenger seat and peered at me through the window. He was a complete stranger whose gaze filled me with fear. It wasn't the surprise of not recognizing him that frightened me; it was what I did recognize — the unmistakable shame in his expression, and the weary temptation that drove him in circles. Before the car behind him honked, he mouthed "hello" and cocked his head. What now? he seemed to be asking. A bold, unbearable question.

I bolted to my feet, slung the gym bag over my shoulder, and hurried toward home. Now and then I turned around to make sure he wasn't trailing me, both relieved and disappointed when I didn't see his car. Even after I became convinced that he wasn't at my back (my sudden flight had scared him off), I kept turning around to see what was making me so nervous, as if I might spot the source of my discomfort somewhere on the street. I walked faster and faster, trying to outrace myself. Eventually, the bus I was supposed to have taken roared past. Turning the corner, I watched it bob eastward.

Closing the kitchen door behind me, I vowed to never leave home again. I was resolute in this decision without fully under-standing why, or what it was I hoped to avoid; I was only aware of the need to hide and a vague notion, fading fast, that my trouble had something to do with sex. Already the mechanism of self-de-ception was at work. By the time my mother rushed into the kitchen to see why I'd returned so early, the thrill I'd felt while waiting for the bus had given way to indignation.

I poured out the story of the man circling the block and pro-tested, with perhaps too great a passion, my own innocence. "I was just sitting there," I said again and again. I was so determined to deflect suspicion from myself, and to justify my missing the class, that I portrayed the man as a grizzled pervert who drunk-enly veered from lane to lane as he followed me halfway home.

My mother listened quietly. She seemed moved and shocked by what I told her, if a bit incredulous, which prompted me to be more dramatic. "It wouldn't be safe," I insisted, "for me to wait at the bus stop again."

No matter how overwrought my story, I knew my mother wouldn't question it, wouldn't bring the subject up again; sex of any kind, especially sex between a man and a boy, was simply not discussed in our house. The gymnastics class, my parents agreed, was something I could do another time.

And so I spent the remainder of that summer at home with my mother, stirring cake batter, holding the dustpan, helping her fold the sheets. For a while I was proud of myself for engineering a reprieve from the Athletic Club. But as the days wore on, I began to see that my mother had wanted me with her all along, and forcing that to happen wasn't such a feat. Soon a sense of compromise set in; by expressing disgust for the man in the car, I'd expressed disgust for an aspect of myself. Now I had all the time in the world to sit around and contemplate my desire for men. The days grew long and stifling and hot, an endless sentence of self-examination.

Only trips to the pet store offered any respite. Every time I went there, I was too electrified with longing to think about longing in the abstract. The bell tinkled above the door, animals stirred within their cages, and the handsome owner glanced up from his work.

*

I handed my father the *Herald*. He opened the paper and disappeared behind it. My mother stirred her coffee and sighed. She gazed at the sweltering passersby and probably thought herself lucky. I slid into the vinyl booth and took my place beside my parents.

For a moment, I considered asking them about what had happened on the street, but they would have reacted with censure and alarm, and I sensed there was more to the story than they'd ever be willing to tell me. Men in dresses were only the tip of the iceberg. Who knew what other wonders existed — a boy, for example, who wants to kiss a man — exceptions the world did its best to keep hidden.

It would be years before I heard the word *transvestite*, so I struggled to find a word for what I'd seen. *He-she* came to mind, as lilting as *Injijikian*. *Burl's* would have been perfect, like *boys* and *girls* spliced together, but I can't claim to have thought of this back then.

I must have looked stricken as I tried to figure it all out, because my mother put down her coffee cup and asked if I was

OK. She stopped just short of feeling my forehead. I assured her I was fine, but something within me had shifted, had given way to a heady doubt. When the waitress came and slapped down our check — "Thank you," it read, "dine out more often" — I wondered if her lofty hairdo or the breasts on which her nametag quaked were real. Wax carnations bloomed at every table. Phoney wood paneled the walls. Plastic food sat in a display case: fried eggs, a hamburger sandwich, a sundae topped with a garish cherry.

Imitation
of Life

~~~~~~~~~~~~

My mother wanted a freezer so she'd always have plenty of meat on hand, an idea my father considered an extravagance. *Loggerheads* was the word she used to describe their discussions about it. I was ten years old, too young to know exactly what she meant, but the word, along with her tone of voice, suggested a blunt, wooden collision. Every morning at breakfast my mother wheedled — "In the long run, Ed, it'll save us money. I can buy good cuts of beef in bulk. It's not like we can't afford it or something. You're the steak lover; I want it for you" — and my father nodded, promised to consider, then buttered his toast and promptly forgot. Or pretended to forget. In retrospect, it seems to me that he enjoyed, with an almost erotic pleasure, the power to pique his wife's desire for a major appliance.

How my father finally gave in, how the Kenmore men fit the freezer through our back door, I don't remember. But I can still see my mother plugging in the cord, her face taut with anticipation. The glossy white box began to hum and shudder — I could feel its vibrations through the floor — an object born to its practical purpose right there in our suburban kitchen. Mother stepped back and hugged herself. Given the magnitude of her satisfaction, it could have been a racecar roaring to life, or a luxury liner drifting from its dock.

It took two days for frost to crystallize on the freezer's interior walls, and my constant lifting of the lid in order to check on its progress caused clouds of cold air to spill from the rim. "A watched pot . . . ," my mother would warn me incongruously, standing at the sink and rinsing dishes. Once the built-in thermometer registered thirty-two degrees Fahrenheit, my mother gathered her keys and her purse and ushered me out the door. She seemed large and hardy with a sense of mission, and we barely spoke as we walked down the street. The air was mild. Tree limbs arched above our heads, mottling the pavement with shadows. At the corner of Normandie and Franklin we passed the house of her friend Molly Gingold, a woman after whom I'd named a cocker spaniel hand puppet because its limp ears and glassy eyes brought to mind Molly's perpetual depression. My mother had tried to explain to me that Abe Gingold had died suddenly, leaving Molly with financial hardships, not to mention lonely nights. Despite my mother's attempts to instill in me a sense of empathy, Molly's presence had an eerie effect, like a record played at a too slow speed. She was watering pots of geraniums on her front porch, the hem of her dress at an odd angle, a dingy crescent of slip exposed. She lifted a lazy hand in our direction. "Wave back," my mother hissed at me under her breath. Even from a distance of several yards, I could make out patches of scalp through the brownish cloud of Molly's hair. "Where to?" called Molly, her voice without inflection. "Meat," my mother shouted gaily, and Molly, having been told, no doubt, the saga of the Kenmore freezer, gave my mother a knowing wink.

During the rest of our walk, I had to submit to a lecture about the importance of kindness. It wouldn't hurt one bit, said my mother, to try at least to be nice to Molly. After all, she'd done nothing to me. What I couldn't explain to my mother was that I reacted instinctually to the sour scent of Molly's depression. The skin drooping from her chin and arms might as well have been misery made flesh. If Molly came near me to say hello, it seemed as if her shadow eclipsed the light, and I had to step back to save myself. But worst of all, I wondered why it was that my mother felt her friend's grief so keenly; was she lonely and inconsolable, too, in ways I couldn't see? "OK," I snapped. "I waved at her, didn't I?"

At Bell's Meat Market, still pouty from my reprimand, I leaned against the slanted glass of the butcher's case as my mother pointed to rib roast, sirloin, porterhouse, and T-bone. The butcher tore off bits of tape and wrapped each piece of meat in white paper. He worked quickly, tabulating the enormous order with the nub of a pencil. The people behind us grew restless, but the sign on the back wall — Now Serving number such and such — stayed the same regardless of their grumbling. After a while, a woman muttered under her breath and a man jiggled the change in his pocket. "I'm shorthanded today," the butcher announced periodically, looking around for his phantom help. I slunk away from my mother, hoping the irritated patrons wouldn't know that I belonged to the woman whose greed was making them late. From my refuge in the corner, I could see my mother evaluating, as if in a trance, the color and thickness and marbling of the meat. Paper packages crackled one atop the other. "Will that be all?" the butcher asked when my mother fell silent.

"I think so," she said.

"You're sure, ma'am?"

"She's sure," erupted someone in the crowd.

My mother turned, fists clenched at her sides. "I have a family to feed," she said, glaring in the general direction of the sarcasm. She was in her early forties, older than the mothers of most of my friends, her forehead scored by faint lines, her angular features blurred by middle age. Wavy hair curled from her head as if she were walking against a strong wind. "You'll have to deliver," she said to the butcher. "I don't drive a car."

*

My mother grew up in the meat-packing district of Chicago. Though she rarely talked about her childhood, the arrival of the freezer stirred her to tell me stories in which sides of beef hung like a leitmotif. Every day on her way to elementary school, she heard the rumble of cattle trains rolling in from outside the city. "Outside the city seemed like a dream," she told me, by which she meant any green vista not cramped with brick tenements, platforms for the El, and vendors hawking their goods from carts. Walking past the cavernous slaughterhouses, she saw funnels of light from hooded lamps, lamps that burned even in daylight, and flayed carcasses swinging from hooks. And the smell. When she tried to describe it, her head drew back and her nostrils flared; she appeared to be assaulted by it still.

She'd lived with her Russian immigrant parents, Harry and Dora, and six brothers and sisters in a coldwater flat, a couple of rooms with views of limp laundry or, if you craned your neck just so, a sliver of iron sky. Her parents were slow in learning the language and bumbled their way through the simplest routines. "See you yesterday," my grandmother was reported to have said to her friends at the end of every conversation, a locution that endured till her death. And my grandfather, more afraid of than awed by modern conveniences, once yelped with fear when a bulb he was screwing into the ceiling bloomed with light in his trembling hand. These quirks were a source of both amusement and embarrassment for the children who spoke fluent English and remembered little or nothing of Russia, a land of such privation and cruelty to Jews, they believed it was their duty *not* to remember.

On the topic of her siblings, my mother became sullen and

remote, saying only that two had died of influenza, one of cancer, and one in an accident the details of which she refused to divulge. Her reverie could have continued, but she trailed off, thinking perhaps that morbid stories about her childhood might make me afraid of my own. The world was steeped in suffering, that much was true, but she believed that silence was the most effective balm, and further questions on my part were futile. Besides, my mother realized this air of silent tragedy lent her the mystique of her favorite movie star, Gloria Swanson, and cast her hurts in a glamorous light.

Only her brother Bernard — I'm his namesake — had survived till my childhood, and she consoled herself with the fact that he had done well enough to at least begin to compensate for their family's misfortunes. The editor in chief of *Family Circle* magazine, he lived thirty minutes away from us in Beverly Hills. He and my aunt Fran threw extravagant birthday parties for their children, and every year they planned a new amusement, a clown or magician or swaybacked pony who suffered many a child in its saddle. Every Chanukah, Bernard and Fran sent me a sweater from Saks Fifth Avenue on Wilshire Boulevard, and my mother, more dazzled by their gifts than I, saved the gold boxes and matching bows long after the sweaters had grown too small. But if Uncle Bernard's wealth, if his triumph over the disadvantages of the past, had a symbol, it was, as far as my mother was concerned, the lanai in the center of his sprawling house. Accessible from a sliding glass door, the lanai consisted of a forked palm tree taller than the roof, and a boulder surrounded by curling ferns. My mother's America, with all its compelling promises, was manifest here, in the tropical retreat where she sometimes sought refuge during noisy parties. "I'll be on the lanai," she'd say, enjoying an excuse to use the word, so full of reverent anticipation she could have been saying *Adonai*. Perched on the boulder, alone and unself-conscious, she'd sigh a deep Semitic sigh and tilt her face toward the sun.

*

Organized as meticulously as a filing cabinet, the freezer held bags of peas, boxes of Popsicles, and tubs of ice cream, but they were relegated to a bin on the side, leaving two-thirds of the space free for the packages of meat. Every day she performed a kind of alchemy, lifting the heavy lid, rummaging for the right parcel, letting the frozen meat defrost on a windowsill above the sink.

If my father had initially met my mother's wish for a freezer with resistance, none of it was evident once he faced a steak, pot roast, or chop. My father and I would spread paper napkins over our laps while Mother tended the stove. Before us sat the tease of condiments: bottles of ketchup and Worcestershire sauce, a statuesque wooden pepper mill. Roasted, fried, baked, or broiled, the rich smell of cooking meat would cause my father to salivate, to hover eagerly over his plate. Once a meal was placed before him, the man ate with ravenous abandon. He chewed so hard he almost forgot to breathe. It was as if he were trying to beat an unreasonable deadline, or was worried that some authority would barge into our house unannounced and confiscate the food before he finished. He barely swallowed one bite before he pierced another, dredging it through the residue of ketchup that smeared his plate like a finger painting.

It was dangerous to look at my father when he was in this state. He was liable to construe any sideways glance as a challenge to his pleasure. Even to smile in vicarious enjoyment would have caused him irritation, like petting a dog who is scarfing his kibble. My father's hunger was edged with desperation; he owned a house, a four-door sedan, his law practice burgeoned year after year, yet despite what he had, it wasn't enough, and nothing, nothing, could fill him up. While he sat there, bent on satiation, my mother puttered at the kitchen counter and I silently chewed the remainder of my meal. He finally left the table weary and mute, a man who had run a mile with his mouth.

Only after my father was gone would my mother sit down with me and pick at the scraps he left on his plate. She swore she was full from tasting the food while making dinner, but she'd suck the bones for morsels of meat and make a noise like a mockery of kisses, her fingers eventually glistening with grease. Sometimes we talked about what I'd done in school that day, or whether I'd liked the dinner enough to have the same dish again. Sometimes she thumbed through back issues of *Family Circle* in search of recipes — meatloaf with oatmeal, crown rack of lamb — stuffing into her apron pocket the ten-dollar bills, her weekly allowance, that my father left at the table like a tip.

*

My mother bought more meat with her allowance. In this way my parents leapfrogged through years of their marriage: money, meat, money, meat. It was a clean arrangement, a tacit contract which didn't require fussy discussions. She cooked in the kitchen. He worked in the world. Together in the evenings, they rarely touched or argued or spoke; the times I'd barged into their bedroom as a child, I'd find two limp, immobile figures occupied by different dreams. My parents shared the same house yet lived in separate provinces, and that, in connubial terms, was that. Still, they continued to care for one another in the manner befitting a husband and wife: she provided him with nourishment, he provided her with cash.

A restless wife who was rich in tips, Mother loved to visit department stores. The problem was, she didn't drive. The reason she gave for never getting a driver's license was that she had been born in Russia and had never officially become a United States citizen. If she went to the Department of Motor Vehicles, she claimed, her alien status would be discovered and — forget parallel parking or the vision test — she'd find herself deported in a snap. Whenever she told me this story, she lowered her voice and toyed with my collar, and our bond felt clandestine, her residence precious, and I'd think of our home as her only refuge from exile in a foreign land as cold as our Kenmore freezer.

Had I known then about naturalized citizenship, had I seen her story as a hedge against the independence a car could offer, I might have argued, might have shamed her into learning to drive. Her elaborate lie should have become apparent to me when she told Molly that she couldn't apply for a driver's license because her birth certificate had been destroyed in the Chicago fire; and yet I distinctly remembered her digging it out from a bureau drawer in order to show me that she was born on the Fourth of July, explaining that she and America shared a common date of birth. In the end, however, I found it satisfying to play a part in her fiction of unbelonging. The melancholy of her possible loss stayed with me like a mild flu, a reminder of our importance to each other. Mother's dutiful, loyal boy, I guarded her secret as zealously as one would guard a priceless jewel.

My reward for protecting her was that I got to go along on shopping excursions, sure to return with some coveted item: a Krazy Straw or Silly Putty. Molly Gingold was recruited to drive. My mother and I would wait outside our house, watching Molly's Oldsmobile inch up the street as slowly as a sunrise. Mother tried to stifle her impatience, checking her watch, patting her hair, fishing in her handbag to make sure she'd brought not only the ten-dollar bills rolled tightly in a rubber band, but Kleenex, dimes for emergency phone calls, and a couple of apples in case we got hungry. My arm would be extended, ready to open the back door long before Molly maneuvered her car next to or, more often, onto the curb.

No sooner was I sprawled on the back seat than all my excitement disappeared. The car smelled inexplicably like hair, or rather like the loss of hair, and I'd notice again that Molly was balding. Could grief cause a person to lose her hair, to forfeit tiny strands of herself? I could only wonder, then keep myself from wondering. It felt rude to see her scalp from behind, the smooth, shiny, private white.

On one excursion, only minutes after we pulled away from the curb, I heard honking and turned around to see several cars clogging the road behind us. Car horns seemed to exist at a decibel outside the range of Molly's hearing, because no matter how loud and frequent the honking, she drove in slow motion and took up two lanes. I felt like a prisoner, trapped in her lassitude, her clumsy meander through time. My mother must have felt anxious too. She touched the dashboard with both hands and gently suggested that Molly move over and let the cars behind us pass. The more lethargic and distracted the chauffeur, the more my mother prodded her to talk. "Speak to me, Molly Gingold," demanded Mother. "Keep trouble inside and say hello to ulcers." Humoring her depressed friend forced my mother (ordinarily a quiet woman, and not exactly an optimist herself) to look on the bright side, to counter Molly's dour remarks with advice, or a joke, or a bromide.

"Sleep is a thing of the past," said Molly, floating over to the side of the road, "like parties and movies." Cars hurtled by, the drivers shooting us angry glances.

There was no arguing with the ashen circles beneath Molly's eyes, but my mother told her to try soothing music, or a snifter of brandy if it came to that. "You need to stay awake to have more time to feel sorry for yourself?" asked Mother. "Don't take your problems to bed, doll, 'cause if you lie down with dogs, you'll wake up with fleas."

Molly nodded quizzically, mired in layers of meaning.

"Besides," said my mother, "if you want to go to the movies, who's stopping you? The National Guard?"

Molly shook her head like a child refusing medicine. "I can't go to the movies alone, Lil. Have you ever gone to a movie alone? Go ahead and try it if you want to feel like a freak of nature. Men in trench coats," Molly added in a whisper, "that's who goes to movies alone."

"Pish! I'm married and I never go to movies. So even if you have someone to go with, you don't necessarily go." Molly needed a sister in disappointment, and Mother gladly volunteered.

"I go to movies alone," I interrupted. Then I told Molly and my mother about the last one I'd seen, *Imitation of Life*, in which Lana Turner's best friend was this really nice Negro woman who was also her maid, and the Negro woman had a daughter who was mulatto but passed for white, but even when her mother was dying, the ungrateful daughter didn't want to be associated with her mother, no matter what Lana Turner and her boyfriend, John Gavin, said or did, for fear that people would know that she was really part Negro.

I didn't mention the fact that I found John Gavin beautiful, or that I wept bitterly all through the death scene.

A long silence followed my outburst, during which my mother and Molly digested the myriad tidbits of plot. "You understood this movie?" my mother asked incredulously.

"Out of the mouths of babes," said Molly, making me mad.

"Anyway," said Mother, turning back to her friend, "the point is that you can't blame everything on the fact that Abe, *alev-asholem*, has passed on. Why don't *we* go to a movie one of these Saturdays?"

"Why not," sighed Molly, her gumption flaring and dying like a match.

But now there was the matter of finding the Broadway's parking lot, and the three of us leaned toward the windshield trying to spot the driveway off Vine that Molly usually overshot, forcing us to circle the block like a dirigible waiting for permission to land. "It's coming," said Mother, wagging her hand at the distance and giving Molly a quarter of a mile to make a slow but momentous lane change. When we pulled into the lot, the parking attendant, having watched our halting progress, offered to park the car himself, saying "free valet" before Molly could protest.

Pushing open the double doors of the Broadway, we stood on a landing several feet above floor level and took in the view. Shoppers milled through a maze of glass-topped counters. Concrete pillars, like gigantic trees, held up the ceiling. Perfumes and soaps and lotions and powders — the atmosphere was glutted with sweetness. The light was diffuse and flattering, the constant roar of buy and sell punctuated by tinkling bells. Instantly my mother and Molly looked younger, their breathing rapid, their troubles doused in scents and sounds.

It took us almost an hour to get to the second floor because, on our way to the elevators, we'd stop and browse. Felt hats sprouted from a metal rack like exotic leaves. Scarves glowed with silky light. If I leaned on a counter long enough, the heat from bulbs lighting the shelves warmed my stomach and forearms. The saleswomen, uniformly soft-spoken and well groomed, didn't seem to mind my presence; some asked if I wanted to sample this or that fragrance, or wanted a gift for "some special girl," by which I thought they meant my mother. In cosmetics, a woman sat on a stool and inclined her face toward a young man who brushed her cheeks with dusky rouge, and I sensed in the forward thrust of her head so much yearning and acquiescence that it embarrassed me to look. Further on, a bin heaped with handbags excited the interest of several shoppers, my mother and Molly (and me) included. "This is pretty, Mom," I said, holding one up; then seized by the terrible shame that only a mama's boy knows, I struck a bored and manly pose, tossing the handbag back like a fish.

By the time we hit the mezzanine, I was ready to go home, or at least to visit the toy department and reap my reward. But Molly and my mother were just warming up, honing their talent to spot bargains, to pick out clothes in the colors and styles best suited for themselves and each other. They moved arm in arm, a tandem intelligence, a single, unstoppable instinct. I followed them past mannequins whose expressions were as blank as dinner plates, whose limbs were twisted into jaunty poses. No sooner would Molly and my mother reach a rack of clothes than they'd be fingering blouses, fanning skirts, reaching their hands up jacket sleeves to feel the lining and extract the price tag. My mother possessed an uncanny ability to sense a salesperson the instant one came within a ten-foot radius. "Just looking," she'd blurt without lifting her head or taking her eyes off the merchandise, and the startled intruder would back away.

While Molly and my mother tried on armfuls of clothes in the dressing room, I plopped into one of those delicate chairs that grow like mushrooms in dress departments. For a while I stared at the pristine walls, footprints in the beige carpet. Corridors to infinity sparkled in a three-way mirror. I knew enough to stay put, no matter how tormented by boredom; left to my own devices, I'd gotten into trouble before. The worst was when I'd wandered into the furniture department and found myself lost in a labyrinth of sofas, dinette sets, and mattresses. I could not, for the life of me, find the escalator, which must have been obscured behind breakfronts and highboys. "Excuse me," I called out, thinking I might be mistaken for a customer instead of a lost child, but there wasn't one adult with a nametag in sight. Muffled by the vastness and hush, my voice sounded especially forlorn, and I saw myself stuck among the trappings of home, but forever alone and displaced. Racing back and forth, desperate for an exit, my mouth became so dry I had to take out my chewing gum and put it in my hand for safekeeping. I'd almost given up hope when I came to an arrow stenciled on a wall, pointing to a stairwell. Reunited with my mother at last, my eyes were red and my nose ran, and the wad of gum had melted in my hand, strings connecting my fingers to my palm like a sticky, ridiculous game of cat's cradle.

I grew hot with humiliation sitting there and thinking about it. And to make matters worse, I knew that my waiting was pointless; disappointed by the width of a collar or the cut of a pocket, Molly and my mother rarely bought anything they tried on. Put off by flaws in their own reflection, they found it easier to blame the clothes than to blame the effects of age.

Unwilling to wait a moment longer, I stood up and, ignoring taboo, stomped inside the dressing room. Big deal, I thought, it's just a hall with little shuttered doors, like the swinging doors to saloons in the movies. I searched beneath each one until I saw my mother's feet, her toes as brown as root beer in her nylons. "Mom," I said in a stage whisper, "hurry up already." No answer. I noticed straight pins scattered on the floor. One more whisper and then I plunged inside where, naked except for a girdle and hose, Molly Gingold screamed. She tried to gather herself up the way a person might try to catch the contents of a spilling grocery bag, unable to hide her crotch and bosom with only two hands. Seeing the folds in her stomach, the veins in her breasts, the ruby gooseflesh of Molly's nipples, the expression of helpless hate on her face, I was all surging current, and couldn't move or speak.

And then I felt myself sucked from the room. Only after Molly slammed the door with her elbow — air rushed through the shutters like a gasp — did I realize my mother had yanked me from behind. Sensing how badly I felt, she touched my cheek with a quick, firm, exonerating stroke before she went in to tend to Molly. A woman peered out from a dressing room, squinted to see if I was a boy, then quickly shut the door.

Over and over Molly said, weeping, "It's just that. . . . It's just that . . ." I stood there and waited for her to tell my mother exactly what, apart from being seen in the not-quite-nude by a ten-year-old boy, made her unable to stop her sobbing. But the unfinished phrase kept skipping like a record, and the revelation never came.

It has taken me thirty years and dozens of my own losses to understand the edginess in Molly's grieving. After the sudden death of her husband, how fiercely she must have resisted surprise, interpreting any unforeseen event as proof that the life she'd been guiding by the reins was wild now, brutish, intrusive. I must have disrupted a moment of peace as she stripped off her clothes and hung them up in that quiet, ivory cubicle, about to try on a new skirt or blouse, turning slowly toward a full-length mirror, hoping perhaps that the woman she saw would look a little less like a widow.

*

Our ride home was silent except for the shush of passing traffic and the rhythmic click of the turn signal. Molly hunkered over the wheel, steering us aimlessly through the streets, stricken with a misery she could neither name nor ignore. My mother stared out the window and brooded, drained of ways to make Molly happy. It was, in a sense, a parting of the ways. My mother had stretched her love to the limit; now Molly would have to fend for herself. As for me, I was convinced that the parking lot attendant wondered what awful thing had happened to cause a woman to flee the store, which only aggravated my already considerable guilt. I didn't mean to do anything cruel, but my best intentions didn't matter, and I took it as the harbinger of a future thick with unwitting mistakes.

Though my mother continued to exchange pleasantries with Molly over the telephone, they saw each other less and less. As long as she was able to talk Molly out of her moods, my mother believed that misery was merely a brief, surmountable state; but Molly Gingold could not be consoled, and my mother was forced to admit defeat, to let sadness have the last word. Without a friend to cure of depression, my mother gradually succumbed to one herself. Dull, abstracted, she smoked too many cigarettes and talked to herself as she rummaged through the freezer. All the lines of reasoning she'd used to help Molly appreciate life now hung from the corners of her empty days, as bothersome as cobwebs.

Cooking and cleaning were not enough to keep my mother occupied or happy, and yet the more hollow domesticity became, the more she claimed to enjoy it. Periods of inactivity alternated with bouts of housework. I remember her swiping rags across the baseboards, flushed and panting when she rose to her feet. She'd whack the pillows on the living room couch, claiming she liked to "fluff them up." When she was idle, Mother smoked and stared into space. Then she'd sing the glories of keeping house and, armed with Windex and Comet cleanser, meat defrosting on the windowsill, she'd swallow gloom and subdue the dirt, feed her family, prove her virtue.

Every day she awoke exhausted, crimped by the limits of her self-perception, requiring a pot of coffee to rouse herself and begin again. After seeing her in her bathrobe one afternoon, hunting for dust, I resorted to hiding her cigarettes and schemed to buy her driving lessons. I even had a driving school in mind; on its cars were drawings of a pony in a sports car, and a motto that touted the value of horse sense. My machinations were useless, of course. It hurt me to see her banging drawers, desperate for a smoke, blaming herself for misplacing the pack. And whenever I broached the subject of a car, Mother Russia loomed on the horizon. Day by day her world imploded. In her isolation, our house must have seemed like a medieval map, a single, knowable mass of land with fog and chaos roiling at its edges.

*

The drawer in which my mother kept her birth certificate also contained photographs that she and my father had given each other soon after they met. In the gauzy focus that was then the fashion, they look softly expectant, newly formed, and the use of diminutives — For Eddie, To Lilly — betrays the shy, initial fondness they both must have hoped would grow into passion. I'm old enough now to know that it is nearly impossible to guess at the private life a couple shares, no matter what your assumptions are from seeing them together, even if you are that couple's son. But my fear is that my parents were bound solely by wedlock's conventions, and beyond their shared stake in a house and a child, they had little reason to be together.

My father never seemed to notice my mother's suffering, or if he did, he took it as an indication of his failure and would not have it, would not let her unhappiness affect him. The house was clean, the meals were hot; this was all the evidence he needed to prove that her sorrow was superficial, a condition that would heal itself with the proper dose of benign neglect. Hired by people on the verge of divorce, he too was exhausted, worn thin by depositions, subpoenas, and trials. Against a backdrop that teemed with betrayal, deceit, and revenge, how could his silent life with my mother stand out as a union in need of repair?

It was during this period that my mother started to fantasize about moving back to the Santa Monica beach where she and my father had lived shortly after they were married. "The fresh air will do you wonders," she'd tell me with such certainty that I could taste the stale air of the present. "What a wonderful way to spend each day, with the sound of the waves. You'd love that, wouldn't you?"

Every mention of the beach was accompanied by a single story, and although the details never varied, Mother's wistfulness grew with every telling: She was in the yard of their first house, feeding a sheet into the automatic wringer. The sun was hot, the surf's ubiquitous hiss in the air, damp linen easing though her hands. A breeze came up and swept her dress, blew her hair till it caught in the rollers. She flailed for the switch, head drawn down toward a tub of gray water, back bending against her will as if in a bow to malevolent luck. Her scalp burned and her neck was wrenched and she yelled for help, thinking there was no one near. Then she heard the motor die, and the pulling stopped, and my father was there, releasing her just in time.

*

Husbandless, Molly was free to reinvent her future. During a lengthy telephone conversation, my mother suggested she contact a travel agent, who in turn set her up with an organization that escorted widows and widowers through Europe. The itinerary — meals, lodging, and transportation — would be planned to the last detail. All Molly had to do was gaze from the window of a tour bus, ooh and aah, and snap a few pictures. The goal of the trip was to pry her from her rut, to spring her from the shabby prison of her habits.

It was difficult to imagine Molly making a left turn, let alone traversing the globe, but she surprised everyone by taking to the notion of travel with the zeal of a convert. Braced by the prospect of shedding the past, Molly was determined to begin again, to make up her fate as she went along. A passport was acquired, luggage bought. Her house was painted and put up for sale.

Despite the fact that she'd always encouraged her friend to be happy, my mother was more than a little envious; Molly had revised herself, had rallied her limited energies. My mother must have wondered whether she'd given up on Molly too soon. And she must have been disappointed that it was the plans of a travel agent and not her pep talks that provided her listless, gloomy friend with the ultimate tonic. A rush of conflicted feeling showed in my mother's face when we passed Molly's house one day on the way to the butcher's. Her eyes grew moist and she clicked her tongue; the shingles, the doors, the trim around the windows, had been painted the color of lime sherbet, as lurid as pastel can get. This color shouted audaciously in the face of a neighborhood that was modest and muted by all accounts. Mother and I froze in our tracks, tried to fit this minty vision with Molly. Was this merely a lapse in taste, or a brazen wave farewell?

If Molly's sadness oppressed my mother, her daring sense of color had the opposite effect. After gawking for a while at Molly's house, my mother took a breath, squared her shoulders, and set out for the nearest bus stop. She told me that we'd changed our plans, the meat could wait. I had to walk fast in order to keep up with her. She split the air like the masthead of a ship, peering into the distance. I inhaled the wake of Palmolive soap and the residue of cigarette smoke wafting from her sweater.

We sat side by side on the hard slats of the bus bench. At our backs, an advertisement for spearmint gum showed a secretary slouched at her desk, but in the daydream ballooning above her head she skated on ice with a handsome man, mufflers flapping behind them with a flourish. Each time a bus bobbed into view, its door folding open, my mother leapt to her feet and asked the driver if he'd get us to Vine. After we boarded the right bus, I stared at the strangers who slept or read or stared into space, each of them snug in the vault of their thoughts. Jostled by the stop and go, Mother and I gripped metal poles, pleased to be leaving our neighborhood behind.

Souvenirs in the shape of local landmarks — the Brown Derby, Grauman's Chinese Theater, and city hall — crowded the shop windows along Hollywood Boulevard. T-shirts were emblazoned with stylized suns, or the beams of searchlights crossing in the night. My mother nudged me, remarked and marveled, as thrilled as a tourist in a foreign port.

We disembarked in front of the Broadway, both of us gloating to have gotten there on our own. As soon as we stepped from the bus to the pavement, we agreed that it was better not to have a third party in tow. Our walk to the front entrance was brisk and lighthearted, as opposed to the slow, unfolding turmoil ("My shoes are killing me," "Where'd I put my car keys?") it had always been with Molly Gingold. Costume jewelry was the first stop, discs as bright as Necco wafers and glittering miniature chandeliers. At the perfume counter, my mother dabbed samples and offered me her wrist until scent was the heady sum of my perception.

It was her idea to cap our adventure by buying me something special for school. On the escalator to the boy's department, I proposed a madras shirt, but my mother said they bled in the wash. She wasn't really listening, though, concerned as she was about getting us off the escalator without injury. She told me the story of a child whose foot became wedged in a step — *chewed*, I believe, was the word she used. Squeezing the rubbery handrails until her knuckles turned white, my mother began a running commentary — "Watch it. Oy. We're almost there" — meant to warn me well in advance of the landing. At the last minute she thrust her arm in front of me, the way she might if she drove a car and was forced to make a sudden stop. This maternal protectiveness would, I knew, make other boys bristle, but I basked in her fuss on the rising stairs and even let her take me by the hand.

Had Sigmund Freud modeled shirts in the boy's department of the Broadway that day, held by the gaze of the woman who bore him, he'd be too content to bother with such theories as "close, binding mother" and "cool, distant father." We were perfectly happy to be together, giving voice to sartorial tastes — who could think of the psychic repercussions? I tended toward the paisleys while my mother preferred the solids, especially white and powder blue, saying those shades were "nice on the eyes." It wasn't until we'd exhausted half the stock that I came across the strangest shirt I'd ever seen. It was the only one of its kind left on a rack of ordinary plaids and stripes. When I parted the hangers to get a better look, my sense of sight was overwhelmed the way it might be when daylight floods a dark theater and obliterates the image on the screen. If yellow could burn, that shirt was burning. I thought of a photograph I'd seen at school that showed the sun through a dozen filters, long fingers of fiery light flaring from its surface. "It's new," came the voice of a salesman behind me. The voice was right; yellow was new in name and sensation; I'd never really seen yellow before. "They call it Day-Glo. It's a special kind of dye. Amazing, huh? We sold out fast." I slid the shirt from the hanger and felt like I was donning a natural phenomenon — a sunrise or lightning — rather than an article of clothing. Even when I wasn't looking down, I was aware of its electric properties, could have sworn the color gave off a faint heat that warmed my torso and upper arms.

My mother was rummaging through her purse, and when she looked up, caught unawares as I walked into view, she froze like a player in a game of statues. I turned in a circle, stiff as a floor lamp, worried that moving too quickly would spoil the effect. "What on God's earth," said my mother. The rasp of astonishment in her voice, the intensity in her eyes, made me feel beautiful, if not quite human. The salesman stood to the side and folded his hands; mother and son and Day-Glo garment were a volatile combination. "Oh, I don't think so. I really don't think so," said my mother. Muffled by awe, her words had no force. She closed her purse, assumed a prim and artificial posture, as though acting complacent might make the color fade. I continued to turn in circles. Nothing I'd ever worn had made me so supernaturally happy, had caused me to feel so exceptional and bold. People would notice, talkers would talk, sleepers would wake from their stupor. "Could you please stop spinning for a minute," said my mother, "and let me get a better look." I walked toward her with measured steps, trying to tease her excitement out of hiding.

"It's Day-Glo," said the salesman.

"It certainly is," said my mother, rubbing the sleeve between her thumb and forefinger. She touched the seam where it drooped from my shoulder. "Honey," she said gravely, "I can tell you want it, but it's much too big."

"The kids are wearing them big these days," countered the salesman, still at a safe distance.

"It's the last one," I said. A switch had been flicked, and I was the filament.

Mother hugged her purse to her stomach. "What I want to know is, where will you wear it?"

"He'll grow into it in no time."

Mother glared at the salesman.

"Everywhere," I told her, with the tremulous dedication of someone taking a vow.

Back on the boulevard, my mother lit a cigarette and scrutinized her son; I'd begged to wear my purchase back home. I carried my former shirt, a dowdy relic I could just as easily have left behind, in a Broadway bag. In the periphery of my vision, I was aware of double takes, lingering glances, the craning necks of passersby. I've come to see that afternoon as an early assertion of my homosexuality, but then all I thought was, Let people look, they thought they'd seen everything till now. But they hadn't seen a shirt that radiated light, that made the spectrum seem incomplete. By comparison the world was prosaic and drab. My shirt called the nature of dress into question. Occasionally my mother would flash an apologetic smile at someone who seemed particularly miffed by my brightness, a smile meant to exempt her from any responsibility.

Just sitting on the bus bench trying to be inconspicuous was impossible. Afternoon traffic was heavy on Hollywood Boulevard. I don't think I imagined being given the once-over by drivers and passengers alike. My mother suffered this ordeal with a thin veneer of patience and good humor. "Smile for the cameras," she said when a sight-seeing bus glided past. Away from the quiet confines of the boys' department, in the roar and grit of the everyday world, my bravery was giving way to self-consciousness. But it wasn't until the bugs began to land that I realized the shirt's full effect.

This must have been late in August because I remember thinking that I could wear the shirt on the first day of school. My mother removed her sweater and bundled it in her lap. Next to me, a woman in a nurse's uniform shielded her eyes against the sun and scanned the distance, looking for a bus. "Oh," she blurted, glancing at my shirt, and I smiled the way I had at a dozen others who'd taken notice, if a little more wearily. "You have . . ." she said, but didn't finish. The nurse pointed to a couple of motionless insects on my sleeve. Nothing like plump and noisy houseflies, these were slivers of tropical green, greener than Molly Gingold's house. I was unsure at first if they were even alive, so still they were, and otherworldly. It's a good thing I wasn't squeamish, because I might have smashed them and stained the shirt. A few more landed on the pocket, but the strangest thing was that I didn't see them fly close and light; they simply appeared from thin air and multiplied before my eyes. My mother had seen me looking down at myself in wonderment so often since I'd tried the shirt on that my bent head and gaping mouth didn't strike her as unusual. I had to poke her arm in order to get her attention, but gingerly, so as not to disrupt the colony growing larger by the second. The instant she faced me, she was gripped by the silence that stifles a person when what they expect and what they see are as useless together as mismatched shoes. By the time she managed to let out a moan, the insect life clinging to my shirt could have been mistaken for a pattern in the fabric.

The nurse checked her white uniform to make sure she wasn't covered with bugs too, and at least one of us was relieved to discover that they exhibited an exclusive preference for yellow. It was then she covered her mouth. All her "I'm sorry"s did nothing to alleviate my embarrassment or lessen her laughter. Thinking that a sudden movement might jar them loose, I bolted to my feet and held my arms out to keep from crushing any bugs that had landed near my armpits. "No!" I shouted when my mother made a move to brush them off with her sweater. Nothing, no one, would smear my shirt. Suddenly a bus pulled up. I was hoping that the gust of wind, the blast of exhaust might knock them off. But the insects clung, abundant and stubborn, drawn to a baffled ten-year-old as though to a monstrous blossom.

"This is our bus!" I heard my mother yelling over the screech of brakes. "This is our bus!"

The nurse turned as she boarded. "You might as well get on," she said, her face still red from laughter.

The bus driver didn't notice anything out of the ordinary, at least not right away. It was only later, when the passengers around us were whispering and pointing, that I saw his eyes, narrowed with concern, in the rearview mirror. Walking down the aisle to find a seat, I could hear quarters clinking in the till, and for one insane second I thought it was the sound of pivoting heads. Everyone looked up, or if not quite everyone, enough people to make me feel, in Molly's words, like a freak of nature. My mother bumped me from behind several times to prod me onward, plunging in front of me to get a seat by the window. No sooner had we sat down than she ordered me to take off my shirt. "What happened, son?" asked a man in front of us. Before I could answer — what *was* the answer? — my mother was running her hand down the placket and deftly undoing my buttons. Out of politeness perhaps, the man turned back. I pushed my mother away. Even though my skinny arms made me modest, I yanked the shirt off over my head. Only one or two of the dozens of bugs were sloughed from the fabric. Half-naked in a public place, I perspired from anxiety, my skin chafed by air and light, by the weight of curious gazes. My mother thrust the shirt out the window.

"I'm sorry, ma'am!" shouted the driver. "Passengers must keep their arms inside the vehicle at all times."

"It's an emergency!" my mother shouted back, shaking my shirt at the end of her arm till she'd flicked off the last recalcitrant bug.

I was too embarrassed to think of it then, but I wonder what the city looked like to my mother — waves of heat rising from the sidewalk, souvenirs in glaring windows, throngs of pedestrians blurred by speed — her solvent life in Hollywood as strange as her impoverished past. And I wonder what the motorists next to us thought when, driving along, minding their business, a woman's arm jutted above them and flailed sixty watts of cloth, insects drifting through the August air like a flurry of green snow.

*

That night at dinner, my mother and I told my father what had happened. I gestured wildly enough to suggest a plague of locusts, every adjective overblown. Mother pretty much stuck to the facts, tempering my account detail for detail. She blushed when I said she'd saved the day. Father stopped chewing, looked at her and looked at me, suspicious, I think, that we'd made it up. So the shirt in question was laid on the table. The three of us huddled near it and stared, primitive people hypnotized by fire. "I'll be," said my father, mouth full of masticated meat. "How —?"

"Who knows," said Mother.

"I love it," I said, yellow burrowing into my brain.

"But what," said my father, "could they put in the paint?"

"The dye," corrected Mother. "They can do anything these days. Anything. I don't even try to understand anymore. You blink and the world is completely different."

*

One day my mother was walking to the bus stop and fainted without warning a few blocks from home. A high whine, a flood of bright light, and the world slipped beneath her feet. She came to her senses on someone's lawn, had no idea if she fell there by chance or had the wits to plan her landing. In any case, the grass was soft and she only bruised her wrist. It would have been worse if she'd fallen on the sidewalk, that much was clear, and so she thanked her lucky stars, picked herself up and walked back home.

In her mid-forties, my mother was just beginning to expand the range of her activities. She kept a bus schedule tucked in her purse. She purchased a wire folding cart in which to wheel the groceries home. She was able to read the postcards from Europe — Molly's wonderment was underscored and peppered with exclamation points — without succumbing to pangs of envy. My mother had become a traveler too, an adventuress in her limited fashion. It must have terrified her to think that some unforeseen ailment, some infirmity, might get in the way of the modest independence it had taken her a lifetime to achieve. And so she pretended her swoon was a fluke, and didn't visit the doctor for months.

Seeing how determined she was to ignore her dizzy spells, my father and I became complicit. We didn't make a fuss; she'd asked us not to. If she paused on the landing to catch her breath, we blamed the heat, the steepness of the stairs. We tried to take her increasing absentmindedness in stride; she'd rush into a room, forget what she wanted to say in midsentence, then turn on her heels and rush away. Sometimes I caught her touching a wall as if to confirm its solidity, or bracing herself on the back of a chair. She lost her balance more and more often, unable to trust the wavering world.

After an electrocardiogram and blood tests, the doctor told her she was suffering from the early symptoms of congestive heart disease, and insisted she quit smoking. It was important for her to avoid overexertion, cut down on caffeine, and eliminate fatty foods from her diet, especially red meat. This regimen, plus daily doses of Digoxin, was the only way to prevent the heart attack he thought inevitable. He asked her to come back the following week, and not to take what he'd told her lightly.

Beginning the day she returned from the doctor's, my mother lived in fear of taxing her heart. She drenched her last pack of Tareytons beneath the kitchen tap. Loud noises had the power to quicken her pulse — an unexpected knock on the door, the backfire of a passing car — so she huddled at the quiet heart of the house. She made her bed on the living room couch rather than forge the stairs. My father hired Dorothy Hill, a stocky, efficient black housekeeper who let herself in three days a week, did the shopping and the laundry, and cooked bland food. My mother was left to the task of relaxing. She wore her bathrobe day and night, and a corona of unkempt hair. The only excitement she allowed herself were occasional games of solitaire and the copies of *Family Circle*, compliments of Uncle Bernard, in which she read about busy lives: "Redecorating Your Bathroom on a Shoestring," "Travel Games for Kids on the Go," "Quick 'n Easy Party Snacks." She thumbed through the magazines in a state of self-imposed calm, looking up and nodding a distant acknowledgment when I left in the morning or returned from school. "That's good," she replied to almost everything I said. My mother no longer allowed herself to worry, and since worry had taken up much of her time, she had plenty of time to coddle her heart.

Though my mother had grown remote in an effort to recuperate, I welcomed the widening distance between us. I was frightened by my powerful attraction to men — I cringed inwardly when someone spoke of "homos" and sneered with disgust — and had somehow gotten it into my head that mother-love was the source, or at least a symptom, of such desire. By avoiding my mother as she avoided me, I too might be spared a painful fate. It seems incredible to me now that I could have absorbed, as if through osmosis, that kind of creaky Freudian logic, willing to turn my back on my mother as a way to make myself straight. But I had gotten to the point where I would try almost anything in order to change, from praying to giving up masturbation. Once, after seeing Pat Collins the Hip Hypnotist on television, I decided to wipe the slate of longing clean. I lay on my bed and counted backward from one hundred, allowing my mind to drain like a bathtub, eyelids growing heavy, heavy. When an itch on my elbow made me lose count, I resurfaced to a conscious state and, having failed at another attempt to reform, played with myself for consolation. I conjured up John Gavin with his blue-black hair, his shoulders as broad as CinemaScope.

I avoided my mother for another reason, too. The ever tightening circle of possibility in which she existed made adulthood seem a diminishment, a succession of blows and disappointments, not the headlong ascent into freedom I'd hoped it would be. That life might rob you of the identity, of the future, you'd come to expect, was a notion too close to entertain. It took me years to see the valor in my mother's convalescence. Her autonomy and stamina had been peeled away layer by layer, yet something essential and stubborn was left. She steeled herself against the odds. She incubated the strength in her chest while playing games of solitaire.

*

The freezer's plenitudes had always reassured my mother that she was prepared for anything. The deprivations, the uncertainties of her girlhood in Chicago, ended there, in the chilly depths of a well-stocked Kenmore. In all the years the freezer took up space in our kitchen, my mother never allowed it to "get low." But now that her diet was restricted to small portions of fish and lean meat, now that Dorothy did the shopping, now that Dad and I ate at McDonald's, it was decided that the freezer should be moved into our garage.

My parents figured they should keep the freezer in case they ever threw a large party. An odd reason, considering my mother was confined to the couch and they hadn't thrown a party in years. As long as the freezer remained within reach, they could hold out hope for a life of shared pleasure, a life overflowing with food and drink and a houseful of hungry friends.

Soon after the freezer was moved, however, my father unplugged it in order to save electricity. He stored tools and cans of paint on top, making the lid impossible to lift. In the dim, mote-choked light of the garage, the freezer was eventually shrouded by dust, a vessel of silence and stale air.

A dinette table was placed in the corner where the freezer had been. It was here that my mother and Dorothy sat and talked, sometimes for the better part of an afternoon. "Sanka?" offered Dorothy. "You're welcome," joked my mother, holding up her cup, and the two of them shook with spasms of laughter. This easy rapport had been slow to develop; at first their exchanges were formal, aloof. My mother was unaccustomed to being waited on; who was she after all these years if not a woman who demurred to others? She could barely bring herself to accept, without a twinge of guilt, the chicken broth Dorothy heated for lunch, as though by carrying the bowl to the couch, Dorothy meant to reproach her for laziness. She'd thank Dorothy without looking up, fixed instead on the amber soup. Dorothy's competence and physical strength constantly reminded my mother that her heart was a muscle subject to failure. She sank at the sight of Dorothy hefting groceries, or carrying immaculate laundry upstairs to a bedroom from which she'd been banished.

If Dorothy sensed that my mother envied her labor, she must have found the sentiment perplexing. Perhaps she worried that her employer's discomfort with the presence of a maid was bound to result in disagreements, regardless of how well she did her job. No doubt it impressed Dorothy as pure foolishness for anyone, given the advantage of her expert assistance, to sit on a couch and bristle.

My own relationship with Dorothy Hill was playful from the outset, though my memories of her unreel in silence; when Dorothy threw me a dishrag to sop up a spilled glass of milk, or I called her attention to a hummingbird darting past the kitchen window, we gestured broadly, as wordless as mimes, always aware that my mother rested in the next room. Between us there evolved a secret vaudeville of mouthed exclamations, intricate charades. *It's hot today* — fanning with hand, mopping brow, tongue extruded. *Where's a pencil?* — licking the invisible implement's tip, scrawling on air. Around my mother, Dorothy was a vector of force, around me, a comrade in quiet antics. Who knows what triviality Dorothy and I were trying to convey when my mother, standing in the portal, stumbled upon our game for the first time. Intrigued by our mugging, she watched for a while before she cinched her robe and asked us what on earth we were up to. Dorothy nearly jumped from surprise. "We didn't want to disturb you," she explained. She shot me a conspiratorial wink. "We were having us a discussion."

Whether my mother felt excluded from our theatrics, touched by our consideration, or troubled to think of herself as the source of a household's silence, from that point on her behavior changed. While Dorothy dusted knickknacks in the living room, Mother ventured hesitant questions, afraid to pry, but determined to stir up conversation. Dorothy didn't need much prodding to talk, and the more she talked, the more boldly my mother, between sips of broth, inquired about her personal life. That Dorothy was forthcoming surprised and flattered my mother; she came to think of herself as a confidante rather than a dependent employer. She turned especially interrogative when it came to Henry, the forklift operator Dorothy was dating. Did he have a sense of humor? Did he show up on time for their dates? Was he the sort of man with whom Dorothy could imagine spending her future? Thanks to my mother's unflagging interest, their affair was updated three days a week. Settled into the best position for eavesdropping, I could reconstruct Henry from bits of description — broad black hands, glittering eyes — and developed a vicarious crush. Every gift was itemized. Every spat was reenacted. Every declaration of love was reported, a gem polished by close observation.

Gossip enlivened my mother's days, provided an absorbing, parallel life, and let her forget her predicament. She followed Dorothy from room to room in order to prolong their conversations, and in this piecemeal, unwitting way, gradually resumed the run of her house. Soon she was not only trailing Dorothy, but walking outside to intercept the mail, or hurrying to the kitchen to sniff the cottage cheese before the milkman drove away. And then there were the afternoons they drank Sanka at the dinette table, polishing silver or cutting out coupons, their task the merest pretext for talk.

The Jensens, a fair-haired, photogenic family who purchased Molly's lime green house, often cropped up in conversation. Dorothy had just begun to work for the Jensens, and she inserted into her tales of their domestic life enough tantalizing pauses and juicy asides to keep my mother riveted. According to Dorothy, Victoria, the youngest Jensen, spent all day playing the same record over and over, a shrill, nonsensical song warbled by Tweety, a cartoon canary. Tweety's manic vibrato made Dorothy half mad, and she had to sing hymns to herself in order to drown him out. "That poor pretty child stays indoors all day," said Dorothy, with contagious amazement. "It's not right," my mother chimed in. "No child of mine would sit around the house all day and sing along with some *meshuggeneh* canary." She and Dorothy shook their heads in disbelief, bolstered by the knowledge that things would be different if the child were theirs. There was fresh air and sunlight, after all, and the benefits of playing with one's peers. Even when they learned that Victoria was autistic, Dorothy and my mother somehow arrived at the conclusion that their superior approach to child-rearing would have prevented her unfortunate condition to begin with. They applied a brusque and simplistic psychology to the problems of our neighbors, then congratulated each other on the miraculous, if imagined, results: marriages were saved, mortgages paid, cases of gout and arthritis cured.

However vain or misguided their advice, doling it out allowed them, in fantasy at least, to impose their wisdom on others, to exercise their power over a world in which a frail Jewish housewife and her talkative black maid were relatively powerless. If their strength and common sense went unrecognized by the world at large, they prized and cultivated these qualities in each other. Although it would be a romantic exaggeration to claim they shared an intimate friendship, a gust of fellowship passed between them, brisk and unmistakable, whenever they were together.

I began to gauge my mother's recovery by how often she worked beside Dorothy, and by her ability to assume progressively more strenuous chores. Sometimes I'd find them coughing together in a great agitation of dust. They took turns washing and drying the dishes, and shared a pair of Living Gloves.

No chore, however, encouraged gleeful teamwork like their attempts at interior decoration. An urge to rearrange the objects atop the coffee table would suddenly seize them and they'd tinker with a mound of wax apples, or fan issues of *Family Circle* in different configurations. Then they'd step back to survey the effect and exchange opinions. Ordinarily, I don't think my mother would have appreciated someone else's decisions when it came to the decor of our house, but home improvement with Dorothy Hill led to deep and rewarding agreements. Every week, they displayed atop the mantel a different species of thing, from candle holders to small pots of ivy, tendrils yearning toward the wide bay window. My bronze baby shoes started to appear in various locations throughout the house, shining on a windowsill or posed midstride on the dining room table, a wandering homage to my feet.

I'm not sure which one of them got the idea to use money as a decorative accent, but one day, while I was walking down the hall, I noticed pennies, nickels, and dimes beneath the sheet of glass that covered the mahogany telephone table. Fleet Mercurys. Stout buffalo. Craggy profiles of Lincoln. There must have been at least three or four dollars in loose change, artfully arranged in circles and spirals. I'd heard about kids buying candy with slugs, millionaires lighting cigars with twenties, but none of this lore prepared me for the monetary phenomena in our hall. I had an urge to lift the glass and steal the change; no matter how pretty and exact the patterns, the coins begged to be pocketed, returned to circulation. The same impulse struck me upstairs where I found Dorothy lifting the glass top of the dressing table while my mother lay a dollar bill in each corner, George Washington facing the wood grain. Then Mother took a turn holding the glass while Dorothy made a few slight refinements. Once the sheet of glass was lowered — reflected light washed over the walls — the bills were flattened like flowers in a scrapbook.

"What are you doing?" I asked them.

"Decoratin'," said Dorothy, in her most matter-of-fact drawl.

"But you won't be able to buy stuff," I argued.

Mother said, "It's here if we need it." Her tone let me know she was not to be questioned; she hadn't set foot upstairs in months, and this was her way of reclaiming the room.

They breathed on the glass and, using shreds of an old sheet, wiped it clean of their fingerprints. We hovered over the table and stared. Bald eagles flaunted their wingspans. Scrollwork rose and broke like waves. From the apex of the pyramids, green omniscient eyes gazed back.

*

After I graduated from college, I visited my parents at least once a month. Often, my mother would ask me to drive her to Smarty's, the shop on Vermont Avenue where she bought the polyester pantsuits that crowded her closet. Bargains, and fashions stubbornly out of step, drew elderly women to Smarty's. The shop was hot and claustrophobic. Sun beat through the tinted windows. Muffled by the hum of a standing fan, voices droned like the sea in a shell. From a chair in the corner, I'd watch my mother pick though the racks, holding up a pastel sleeve to test the hue against her arm. "That one's pretty, Mom,"

I'd tell her, thinking that every suit looked the same — bland, synthetic, "nice on the eyes."

To tell the truth, my mother looked a little mannish in pantsuits. Her body had grown squat and shapeless with age. As a result of arthritis, she developed a tough, determined gait. She wore her hair short toward the end of her life. "Hair's easier this way," she'd say, as if vanity and its elaborate hairdos were an unaccountable phase from her past. As a last concession to the feminine, she dyed it a bright, unnatural orange.

Thanks to a regimen of heart medication, she'd lived to mock her doctor's predictions. Though still unfulfilled by the rigors of housework, she considered it a form of exercise, a way to fill otherwise idle hours. Wielding a vacuum or spritzing Windex, she tottered up and down the stairs.

By then, Dorothy and Henry were living with their daughter, Dee, on West Adams. During her last days in my mother's employment, Dorothy couldn't hide her excitement; she'd given notice months in advance, counting down the days aloud until she became a housewife. "I might," she told my mother, "have to hire me a maid."

If anyone appreciated the need for autonomy, it was my mother. She was happy for Dorothy, even though, from her point of view, keeping house was an ambiguous blessing. But my mother loved to listen to Dorothy, to trail in her garrulous wake, and had paid for the pleasure of her company as well as for her labor.

Without Dorothy to inform her about the local goings-on, my mother remained apart from the women and children who peopled our street. Except for a wave and occasional small talk, the neighbors were too busy washing cars or mowing lawns to spend much time with the lady in the pantsuit. Family dramas had to be guessed at from echoes: garbled shouting, urgent knocking on a nearby door, a canary screeching his crazy refrain. That is, if my mother, sipping Sanka at the dinette table, rows of playing cards spread out before her, were inclined to pay the noise any mind.

Her feelings for my father continued to dwindle. She had no hope of recapturing their past or improving their future, yet she wouldn't budge from their life together, thriving on crumbs of wifely routine and the weekly allowance left on the table. In his mid-sixties, my father refused to give up his practice. He left the house every morning at eight and returned too tired and contentious to speak. After eating whatever was set before him, he retreated to the king-size bed.

Molly Gingold had lived in Bellflower ever since her trip to Europe. Mother felt that efforts to help her friend were never properly appreciated, and except for a rare, wistful mention, Molly vanished from my mother's life.

Now and then, Aunt Fran and Uncle Bernard picked my mother up and took her to Bullock's Wilshire, where they lunched on dainty sandwiches as gaunt women modeled dresses and hats. But the outings ended by three o'clock, leaving her stranded in the afternoon. When I called my mother and asked what was new, she never had much to tell.

I'd been renting a small apartment in West Hollywood and supported myself by working at the Paradise Packing Company, a men's shoe store on Santa Monica Boulevard. The store stayed open late in order to attract customers from nearby bars, boutiques, and narrow, deafening restaurants. It was not unusual for me, on the stroke of midnight, to find myself at a stranger's feet, flattering his choice of, say, a pair of cordovan loafers, or cupping his heel with a shoehorn. I was twenty-five, single, afraid I might live alone forever, settling for the touch and attentions that salesmanship required.

On a Friday night in August, after the last customer had gone, I tallied cash and checks in a ledger, nestled shoes back into their boxes, and flicked off the lights. I felt no apprehension of loss, had no idea that my mother's heart had stopped, her eyes going still in the middle of a dream, a wince momentarily tightening her features. For all its concerted, purgative force, her last exhalation went unheard. Father tugged at his bedclothes, shifted position, unaware that a sound had ruffled his sleep, the body beside him losing its heat.

Locking the door to the shoe store behind me, I walked through the color and rush of commerce, saw darkness stained by neon signs. Men in T-shirts milled on the sidewalk, poured from doorways. They had to shout to be heard over the throb of disco music; women wailed, seductive, defiant, each of their stories confirmed by a chorus. The night was warm, impending, alive, as if longing itself were an aspect of the air, like humidity or wind.

Arson

~~~~~~

From the moment I learned about come-as-you-are parties, I wanted to throw one. Birthday parties, picnics, and costume balls paled by comparison. I couldn't shake the image of guests — relatives, teachers, friends from junior high — converging on my house. I pictured them coming from all directions, from apartments and parks and places of business, drawn from every type of routine. One person lifted a cold forkful of dinner to his lips. Another raised a flyswatter, though a fly was nowhere in sight. The vain cashier from Woolworth's wore curlers. The authoritarian crossing guard was wrapped in a baby blue bath towel. Propriety, modesty, and just plain embarrassment made them move as slowly as sleepwalkers, and still they came, some of them grumbling, some of them pointing with glee at one another, a dowdy battalion in underwear and housecoats who forged through the city streets toward my door.

The image of this party was so vivid and gratifying that several times a day I imagined picking up the telephone and dialing guests. "Hello," I'd say, as though nothing were out of the ordinary. And then I'd blurt the startling news, "I'm having a come-as-you-are party!" I suppose it was a kind of egotism or wishfulness to assume that people, regardless of their outfit or grooming, would drop what they were doing and appear in public, shedding their inhibitions just for me.

In retrospect, I can't help but see this obsession as the odd blossom of my loneliness. My mother was preoccupied with house-work, my father with the practice of law. Most of the neigh-borhood kids were on vacation or attending summer school. The light that summer was direct and unrelenting, the afternoons vast. Left to my own devices, steeped in a restless imagination, my solitude was nearly constant.

The come-as-you-are feeling often welled up in me as I was getting ready for bed, brushing my teeth, or staring at my naked body in the bathroom mirror. What, I wondered, were other people doing or feeling at that moment? Were they mesmerized by the weight of their limbs, by the heat of their skin, by the sight of their wrinkled genitalia? Why did my particular mind exist in my particular body? It was difficult to believe that anyone else beheld themselves with such abject and melancholy astonish-ment. In the bright isolation of the bathroom, as the neighbor-hood around me settled into the anonymity and silence of the night, I most desperately wanted a glimpse into the privacy of others.

That summer I began making regular visits to the model homes of Los Feliz Estates, a nearby tract in the Hollywood Hills. None of the real estate agents seemed to notice or mind a thirteen-year-old wandering through the rooms. Sometimes there would be a lull in the number of prospective buyers and I would find myself virtually alone, able to part the drapes or fur-tively flush a toilet. But no act thrilled me as much as coaxing open a desk or bureau drawer. I knew these houses didn't belong to anyone real. I understood that the rooms were furnished to give the illusion of home. Yet every time I opened a drawer — heart racing, breath held in check — I expected to find some contraband, some evidence of a stranger's life: a rubber, a Tam-pax, a diary, money stuffed in a sock. What I found instead was emptiness and the faint, escaping scent of wood.

In the bottom drawer of the built-in bureau in my bedroom, I kept hidden a small collection of pornography, magazines with almost apologetically innocent names like *Pony Boys!* and *Buddies*. The young men between the covers, with their glistening pectorals, backs, and thighs, appeared to have been marinated in oil. One sunned on a rock. Another sprawled on a plaid couch, his nakedness accentuated by the banality of his surroundings. A few studio shots featured moody lighting and classical props — a plaster column, a Grecian urn — and in case there remained any question of artistic intent, each model's crotch was sheathed in a loin cloth. Only rarely were two men shown in the same photograph, and even then they never touched; any heated contact between them was something the viewer inferred. For the most part, each man waited for admiration on his solitary page. Arms tensed, stomachs sucked in, they invited the camera's scrutiny. Their brazenness excited me as much as their physiques.

Not a day went by without my fretting that the magazines, and therefore my desire for men, might be discovered. Finding a foolproof hiding place became nothing short of a criminal pursuit, and before I'd finally decided on the bottom drawer of the built-in bureau, my illicit library had been stashed in an old Monopoly box and wedged beneath the mattress. No sooner would I find a new hiding place than I'd picture that place being violated. Suppose my mother decided to air the mattress one day? Suppose my father got the urge to play Monopoly? The dread of being discovered even seeped into my dreams; I'd be blithely chatting with a policeman, say, when I'd realize to my horror that, instead of wearing my usual clothes, I was wearing the pages of *Pony Boys!*

Eventually, the drawer of the built-in bureau seemed like a risky hiding place, and I thought it might be safer to keep the magazines *behind* the drawer. I took hold of the brass knobs and slid the drawer out with the stealth of a burglar, nervous that my mother, puttering in the kitchen directly below, might hear me and become suspicious. It's entirely possible that I took further precautions, like locking my bedroom door or turning on the transistor radio, so thoroughly did the fear of exposure control me in those days. My anticipation mounted as the lowest drawer inched toward me on its tracks. When it finally popped out of the wall and landed with a muffled thud on the carpet, it left a rectangular hole behind it. I bent down, peered inside. It was as if I'd pulled back the skin of the house and could glimpse the bones and organs within. Two-by-fours and rolls of tar paper lined the floor. Here and there, drips of plaster and paint were preserved in a secret museum. Dry rot had turned patches of wood velvety and uneven. The surface of a pipe a few feet away glinted in the sudden flood of sunlight, and from it issued the sound of water like a sudden rush of breath.

From then on, every time I removed the drawer and reached for my cache of naked men, I saw the darkness at the core of our house and suddenly doubted the white walls, the tidy rooms in which I lived.

To be homosexual was to invite ostracism and ridicule, and I would have done just about anything to escape my need to masturbate to images of men. I bargained with myself, made promises not to, devised equations of abstinence and reward. *Today is Monday; if you don't touch yourself till Saturday, you can go to Woolworth's and buy that model of a '65 Corvette.* But no sooner would I muster my resolve than I'd find myself in a haze of amnesia, a couple of magazines spread before me, opened to my favorite pages. Sometimes it seemed that the only antidote for constant shame was the forgetfulness of orgasm, my body crumpled in a fit of overflowing, every sensation obliterated except for pleasure.

In an effort to control, once and for all, my helplessness in the face of lust, I retrieved, from the same bureau where I stashed the magazines, a pair of plastic handcuffs I hadn't played with in years. Somehow, I got the idea to hook them to my wrists whenever the impulse to masturbate was about to overwhelm me. The reasoning that followed my literal self-restraint went something like this: *O.K. You've done everything you possibly can to prevent it. If it happens, it happens, and you can't blame yourself.* And then I went at it while wearing the handcuffs. In this way I policed my own desire, kept guilt and shame at bay with a toy, and stroked myself with impunity. But it wasn't long before this ritual lost its power to ease my conscience, and soon I started to feel absurd, as though I were wearing a set of matching bracelets, and the plastic links seemed pitiful and weak, and I imagined someone barging in my room and finding a boy, bound by the wrists, unable to resist himself.

I bought the pornography at a store that sold candy, key chains, batteries, dusty artificial flowers, and tabloids in foreign languages. I discovered it by accident one afternoon while walking up and down Western Avenue in search of a Mother's Day card. The place was run by a woman whose eyes, magnified by thick glasses, seemed to follow you wherever you went like the gaze in certain portraits. Her eyes were deceptive, though, because she never seemed to care what happened in her store. Perched atop a stool behind the counter, she rarely moved except to sigh, her posture wilted by boredom. There were times I thought it would be a breeze to sneak past her into the alcove that contained the pornography and simply steal the magazines I wanted. That way I wouldn't have to endure the humiliation of having to buy them, terrified she might ask my age, my hands shaking as I counted out change. Instead, I tried to ignore her, to act nonchalant as I strode toward the shelf where women licked their lips and played with their nipples. My habit was to peruse at least one or two of the girlie magazines before I moved on. I flipped through a blur of bleached hair, arched backs, and breasts rising from frothy lace bras. I probably even convinced myself that, blood humming from sheer fright, I was actually kind of

excited by women, but drawn to men just a little more. Once I'd
looked at girlie magazines long enough to give the impression —
to whom, I wonder, since there was rarely another customer in
sight — of genuine interest, I'd drift toward the rack where I
invariably wanted the first magazine I laid eyes on. Whoever was
on the cover — a man washing his car in the nude, sweat beading
on his tattooed chest, soapy water dripping down the fenders —
he was too beautiful a vision to contain. I couldn't look for long
before my mouth went dry and my skin began to itch.

The mechanics of the sale were clouded by panic. But the last
thing I saw before I left the store were the big omniscient eyes of
the proprietress, like the eyes of God, brilliant with judgment,
peering from a mortal's head.

Back in the silence and privacy of my room, I noticed that one
corner of the brown paper bag which held my purchase was
moist and soft from the sweat from my palm, as though it had
turned to suede. Only then would it occur to me how ferociously
I must have hugged, gripped, shifted the package from hand to
hand as I hurried home, frightened the bag might rip wide open,
afraid I'd run into someone I knew. Sitting cross-legged on the
floor, I extracted the magazine from its wrapping and turned the
pages, only a little more calmly than I had in the store. Once I'd
gained an overall sense of the contents — how many men were
featured, were they smooth or hirsute, husky or thin, was there
some sort of story or theme involved? — I began again from the
first page. This time I went more slowly, evaluating, savoring,
finally choosing the most beautiful man. By then I couldn't stand
more excitement and, faint from the whole clandestine ordeal, I
peeled off my pants. Climax came quickly, and the instant it did,
the mass and shadow of the model's physique seemed to bloom
into three dimensions, and my own body, in a fever-dream of
want, became more real along with his.

Only after masturbation was there room for remorse; it

flooded in to take the place of satisfaction. Every time I so much as glanced at one of those magazines my appetite for men was confirmed, and it stung me to think that the price I'd have to pay was the world's condemnation. How could such an awful penalty result from such exquisite sensation? I can't, to this day, imagine what childhood would have been like without the need for secrecy, and the constant vigilance secrecy requires. The elaborate strategies, psychic acrobatics. You ache for a way to make sense of your nature. You dive headlong into the well of yourself. And no matter what plans you hatch, promises you make, no matter what you do to erase your desire, you feel incorrigible and aberrant before you even know the meaning of the words. Every day you await disgrace. You look for an ally and do not find one, because to find one would mean you had told. You pretend to be a person you are not, then worry that your pretense is obvious, as vulnerable to taunts as the secret itself. In a desperate attempt at self-protection, you shrink yourself down to nearly nothing, and still you are there, as closed as a stone.

*

One Saturday toward the end of summer, a few days before school started, my parents were invited to a brunch in Orange County. My mother baked a chicken breast and left it in the refrigerator in case I got hungry while they were gone. My father cleaned out the car and checked the yard a couple of times to make sure he'd turned off the sprinklers. They departed with an unusual amount of ceremony, telling me they might not be back till late, asking me if I'd be OK. This show of concern might have been what made their leaving seem especially momentous. And opportune. Seconds after the Oldsmobile pulled out of the driveway, it occurred to me that I could purge my life of tempting possessions. Start from scratch in the eighth grade. Wipe clean the slate of longing.

Most of the bonfires I'd seen were in beach blanket movies. Teenagers did the twist and the watusi while flames raged and crackled on the sand. A bonfire seemed as effective a way as any to do the job; heat would scorch the photographs, turn the pages to flecks of ash. My first thought was to set the fire in the middle of the backyard, away from the plump hibiscus bushes and wooden lawn chairs. But the grass was still wet from the sprinklers, and I figured the flames wouldn't take. I could grill each magazine on the barbecue, then pour the ashes into a trash can. But suppose a neighbor poked his head above the fence to see what curious meat was cooking. The whole outdoors seemed too . . . overt. I needed a more protected place.

The garage made sense mostly because my father's car was no longer in it, and it seemed logical — if a boy's tormented, overeager inspiration could be called logical — to take advantage of the Oldsmobile's absence. The floor of the garage was cement, after all, and wouldn't burn. I could close the heavy wooden doors, yet still see what I was doing by the light of the two small windows on opposite walls. Except for my father's workbench and the Kenmore freezer my mother no longer used, the high-ceilinged garage was practically empty.

Match, magazines, empty garage! I waited fifteen or twenty minutes to make sure my parents were good and gone. Walking from room to room, the house seemed huge and plush with quiet — antimacassars draped the chairs like giant snowflakes — and I grew more resolute with every step.

When the moment was right, I dashed upstairs with a grocery bag and yanked the drawer out with such force it slammed into my knees. I groped around, grabbed the seven or eight magazines I owned, and crammed them into the bag. Should someone see me in my journey across the narrow breezeway that separated the house from the garage, I could tell them I was taking out the trash. On my way to the back door, I stopped at the kitchen cabinet where my mother kept a veritable gallery of ashtrays — she'd recently started smoking again — and several boxes of wooden matches. I snatched an entire box, but made a mental note of its exact position on the shelf so that I could replace it without causing suspicion. How proud I was of my foresight, glad that my knack for deception had finally come in handy.

Standing inside the garage, facing outward to pull closed the double doors, I could see the crest of the Hollywood Hills rising against the horizon. In the midday sun, the windows of distant houses glowed like yellow embers. As soon as the doors were shut, the cavernous room grew sheltered and cool. I waited for my eyes to adjust, and then my renewal was under way. I piled the magazines in the middle of the room where puddles of oil, left by the Oldsmobile, stained the floor; in the dim light, they looked as deep and primeval as pools of tar. I paused a moment to contemplate how best to start the fire, and it was then I noticed the men at my feet, their bodies seductive, tight, exciting. But I'd gone too far to stop what I was doing. When I struck the match on the side of the box, the rasp and stench of sulfur made me shudder.

For the first second, everything went according to plan. Touching a match to the first magazine, I felt a sense of profound relief that I wouldn't know again until years later when I actually touched a man. The exclamation mark at the end of *Pony Boys!* caught fire and flared, igniting in turn another magazine on which a sailor wore only bell-bottom trousers. I thought he too would go up in flames, but instead, a trail of smoke curled lazily and disappeared. The fire went out before it had begun, and I had to rethink my approach.

On his cluttered workbench, my father stored the can of lighter fluid he used to start the barbecue charcoal; I found it without the slightest trouble, as though some prodding, superior force had placed it smack in my path. I removed the cap, aimed the metal spout toward the pile of pornography (which seemed to grow larger the longer it took to destroy) and squeezed a thin jet of fuel on top, saturating every page. Vapors assailed me, and with them came associations of afternoons in our backyard, Mother molding the hamburger patties that my aproned father would flip with aplomb, his aluminum spatula catching the light. What a disappointment to return to my senses in a dank garage, the doors shut tight against prying eyes, the most incriminating objects I owned heaped in an acrid, sopping pile.

This time I stood back and tossed the lit match, having wits enough to understand that unless I kept my distance, my eyebrows and hair were in danger. But nothing could have prepared me for the whoosh that followed, a whisper of swift consumption. I recoiled from the blast of heat. The walls around me tinted red. Flames shot several feet into the air, some of them as tall as I was. From their flickering tips coiled strands of black smoke that streamed toward the ceiling and spread across it, as ominous as thunderheads. Even if the fire eliminated my collection of men, what if there remained a thick, telltale smudge on the ceiling of my parents' garage? I floundered by firelight, plucked from the realm of possibility a dozen useless excuses: *A can of insecticide had exploded; I tried one of Mother's cigarettes.* And while I was at it, the puddles of oil began to burn, and my bonfire reached its peak.

The first scrap of anatomy was a man's arm. It fluttered down like a molted feather, part of a picture singed at the edges. Legs and shoulders and buttocks came next. The magazines were burning to pieces, and the pieces, lifted on sudden updrafts, were raining everywhere. I swiped at the stifling air, trying to catch a couple of muscles. When it finally dawned on me that things were getting worse instead of better, I leapt in and out of the fire in a sorry effort to stomp it out. In the periphery of my vision, I saw my shadow loom up on the walls, all wavering agitation. I

slapped at my smoldering shoelace, plucked at the cinders landing in my hair. The more I stomped on the hot spots, the more
the bodies multiplied, a flurry of glowing male flesh. And just
before I managed to smother the fire, in a single wracking spasm
of guilt, I imagined my picture on the evening news, and the
blackened rubble of our former home.

Even after the flames had been extinguished, there was smoke
to contend with. The garage was filled with hazy, unbreathable
air. Throwing open the double doors, I half expected to see fire
trucks arriving, or the neighbors lined up in a bucket brigade. I
was stunned to realize that it was still a Saturday afternoon, the
sky clear, the hills unscorched. Smoke billowed over my head and
drifted into the placid sky. I ran to the edge of our driveway and
breathed deeply, as though I were preparing to dive into water,
then ran back inside. I flung open the two small windows and
used the grocery bag to fan away the remaining smoke. Coughing, eyes watering, I came out for air once more, turned on the
spigot and wrestled the garden hose around the side of the house
and into the garage. Though fairly certain the fire was out, I
doused the mound of burnt magazines.

Getting rid of the smoke was a cinch compared to the bits of
men's bodies. My dread of the magazines being discovered in my
bedroom was nothing compared to the dread that I'd never lo-
cate all the fragments of anatomy lurking who knows where. A
handsome head had landed near a jar of nails on my father's
workbench. A naked gladiator, nearly complete, wedged himself
in a terra-cotta pot. I imagined my parents pulling up in their
Oldsmobile, quizzically sniffing the stale air and finding pieces of
male physique inexplicably stuck to their shoes. My hands were
black by the time I finished scrutinizing every square inch of the
garage, groping behind the freezer, hoisting myself up on a step-
ladder to check the high shelves of the workbench. I scooped
every stray appendage into the grocery bag, which I stuffed at the

bottom of a garbage can, realizing too late that I should have simply wrapped up the magazines and thrown them away in the first place. Examining the ceiling with a flashlight, I convinced myself that my father wouldn't notice the vague gray shadow that, if pressed, I would blame on car exhaust. I considered spraying the garage with the can of air freshener my mother kept in the guest bathroom, but wouldn't lilac smell as suspicious as smoke? I swept the wet ashes into a dustpan. Then I had to scour the dustpan. Then I had to wash the bristles of the broom. Then I had to bleach the kitchen sink.

My clothes were permeated with smoke and smudged with soot, and I decided to stuff them behind the drawer where I'd hidden the pornography until I could figure out how to clean them without risking my mother's questions. My tennis shoes required an entirely different, but equally anxious, set of ablutions, and after I cleaned them I wadded the paper towels into tight balls and threw them away. Even the washrag with which I cleaned my face had to be examined for traces of soot. It was as if I were leaking a dark, persistent misery, tainting everything I touched. For the rest of the afternoon and into the evening, every time I closed my eyes I saw a phantom of the conflagration, as if I'd been branded by its afterimage. Trying to divert myself with records and books, I would periodically stop what I was doing and, as though jarred awake by a bad dream, sniff the clothes into which I'd changed, or search my skin for particles of ash, seized by the apprehension that I hadn't covered my tracks.

My parents were oblivious to the crisis when they returned home after dark. They must have had a couple of drinks at brunch; my mother's cheeks were flushed, and my father blinked slowly as he told me what they ate. I listened intently, asked several questions. Who else was there? Did they play any games? I wanted to distract them from my act of arson, but I was also soothed by the details of their party, a tale of mingling, ease, and indulgence.

That night, while getting ready for bed, it became clear to me that attempts to reform myself would prove every bit as disastrous as staying the same. The ruined clothes behind the drawer; the grocery bag at the bottom of a trash can — now I had even more to hide.

*

The guest list for my party consisted of Jack Pearlstein and Richard Levine, two boys I knew from synagogue and junior high. Though unrelated, Jack and Richard might have been mistaken for brothers; they both possessed alert brown eyes and wavy hair. They also lived in the same stucco apartment house. Athletic and friendly, Jack and Richard were slow to exploit their physical power. We sometimes ate lunch together in the school cafeteria or walked home as a raucous trio. Jack and Richard shared a repertoire of phrases. "Yes, Mother dear," one of them would drone whenever the other offered advice. "Pip, pip," in an arch English accent, greeted any pretentious remark. They both called me Cooper instead of Bernard, this formality having the paradoxical effect of tenderness.

Because we'd once studied Hebrew together in preparation for our bar mitzvahs, Jack and Richard considered me, in the broader context of the junior high, an equal member of our ethnic subset, though I was nothing like them in temperament or strength. They teased me good-naturedly about my tendency to daydream and equivocate — "Earth to Cooper, come in Cooper" — and for the first time my reticence seemed like an eccentricity rather than a flaw. A boy, for once, among boys, I relied on their attentions — back slaps, mock blows, gross jokes — for a taste of normalcy, attentions made especially tenuous and sweet because I suspected that Jack and Richard would turn their backs on me if my secret were revealed.

I'd hardly seen either of them that summer. They'd been working together as counselors at a camp for Jewish youth outside Los Angeles. Figuring they'd be home by now, I dialed Richard first. "Uh-huh," he answered the phone, as though it were the middle, and not the beginning, of a conversation. We caught up on news of the summer with the halting, blasé phone persona of adolescent boys. And then, unable to restrain myself, I sprang my surprise. "A what?" asked Richard. After I explained the premise of the party, he told me that he was wearing shorts and a T-shirt. In my zeal to get the party under way, it had somehow slipped my mind that if I wanted to have the guests arrive in compromising clothes, it would be pointless to call them at two in the afternoon. I had to improvise, to bend the rules, and in what Richard himself might have called "a save," I asked him to come to my house the next day, but to wear what he wore to bed that night. "Whatever," he said. Then I phoned Jack and asked the same.

The sheer intensity of my anticipation embarrassed me long before the guests showed up. The day of the party, dressed in a pair of powder blue pajamas, I set up my hi-fi in the living room and recruited my mother to make a platter of sandwiches, aware that the outfit made my fuss seem all the more fruity. Circling the living room, I searched for something to touch or rearrange that would make the prospect of fun more likely. Wax apples were adjusted, pillows plumped. I chalked my excitement up to the fact that this was the first party I'd given on my own, and not to the fact that two boys I idolized were due to arrive at my house any minute, looking like they had just rolled out of bed. Over and over, I imagined the hilarity that would ensue once the doorbell rang, Jack in his underwear, Richard in his bathrobe. Even if I couldn't have put it into words, the metaphysics of the party weren't lost on me: wrenched out of context, together in our bedclothes, we would be more alike than ever before.

The sound of the bell made my heart pound, and I had to take a moment to compose myself before opening the door. Standing side by side, the Hollywood Hills rising behind them, Jack and Richard wore the same chinos, short-sleeved shirts, and scruffy Keds they wore to school. The effect was as jarring as a bride in a bikini. "Did we wake you?" asked Jack, the two of them doubling over with laughter. I forced myself not to show any signs of anger or disappointment. "Very funny," I said, ushering them inside. They made a beeline for the sandwiches. Hot with shame, I raced upstairs to change. "Cooper," Richard shouted after me. "We came as we are."

"Yeah," I yelled back, "a couple of jerks."

"Honey," I heard my mother call from the kitchen, "I think your friends are here."

Mouthfuls of tuna muffled Jack and Richard's snickering.

The few seconds I'd spent in their presence were almost as bad as the dream in which I wore the pages of *Pony Boys!*, proof I was skewed, forever out of sync. I threw on my school clothes, but the change seemed futile, like dressing a chimpanzee in a suit to make him look human. Returning to the living room, I silently berated myself for going through with such a stupid idea in the first place and wished I'd never opened the door. Could I make them think it was a bad joke? What I'd wanted all along, it occurred to me, was a girls' party, with lots of gossip, dancing practice, and lolling about in pretty pajamas. Worried that the slightest sound or movement might give away my girlish urges, I sat on the sofa and turned to stone. Ten minutes into the festivities, and it was already obvious that laughter and astonishment weren't likely to materialize. The sandwiches were almost gone. The prospect of fun had deflated like a balloon. The wheels of the party spun in a rut.

Jack and Richard asked what we were going to do besides listen to records. Every so often one of us would throw out an idea, which the other two would instantly veto. No, I protested, a little too loudly, when one of them said, "Monopoly?" Our indecision lumbered on and on, and I stared through the picture window at the smoggy summer day. We finally decided to venture outside, snatched a pack of my mother's cigarettes, and left the house.

Refugees from a defunct party, we roamed the neighborhood. The heat made us too listless to accomplish anything more than petty mischief. Jack threw a rock and chipped the flank of a plaster deer. Richard flipped up the red flags on a few mailboxes. I showed them how you can squeeze the buds of drooping fuchsias to make them pop like cap guns. After a while we sat down on the grassy bank of someone's front yard, beneath the shade of a carob tree. The three of us lit cigarettes and pretended to smoke like veterans. Richard blew loose, short-lived smoke rings. Jack picked flecks of tobacco off his tongue and flicked them into the air. I took a long, labored drag, then held up my cigarette. "Filter tips," I said in a disgruntled baritone. "You could get a hernia from the draw." This was something I'd heard on TV, but Jack and Richard laughed in approval, and I felt the remark had restored me in their graces. Soon our cigarettes collapsed into ash. Dizzy from smoke, unable to speak, the three of us lay back on the lawn and stared at sunlight swimming through the leaves. Pressed against the turning earth, dry grass crackled behind my ears. My friends breathed deeply on either side of me, two strapping, affable boys.

*

Life in the eighth grade was not very different from life in the seventh. Jack and Richard and I stuck together at school, yet no matter how well we got along, agreed on pop tunes, or copied homework, my secret remained a threat to our allegiance. My parents began to seem like people whose love I'd lose if they really knew me, and I viewed their habits — Mother washing dishes in the kitchen, Father rushing off to work — with a premature nostalgia. In the absence of pornography, I could ferret out the male flesh in *Reader's Digest*, *Look*, and *Life:* ads for aftershave, VapoRub, and vacations in Bermuda.

I no longer thought about throwing a come-as-you-are party, but my wish to see into private lives, to witness what the world kept hidden, would not disappear. The more fiercely I guarded my inner life, the more I loved transparency and revelation. I wanted the power to read people's minds. Radar hearing. X-ray eyes. I pored over a book at school in which layers of anatomy — tissue and organs and skeleton — lifted away as the pages were turned. Pat Collins the Hip Hypnotist was my favorite act on TV; she persuaded her subjects to shed their inhibitions, and they bawled like babies, barked like dogs. Charles Atlas, maker of he-men from weaklings, flexed his muscles in comic books, and there were times I stared with such fixity that I could see the tiny dots of the print, as if I were glimpsing the man's very atoms.

Almost Like
Language

∿∿∿∿∿∿∿∿∿∿∿∿

I didn't know I was stoned until the eggs I was scrambling began to look like a storm at sea. Staring into the bowl, I lost track of time and whisked the fork around and around, mesmerized by foamy yellow waves. When I looked up, Greg was shaking with laughter; he held a frying pan in one hand and with the other pointed at me. Just moments ago I'd told him that the joint we smoked had no effect on me at all. My mouth wasn't dry, my feet weren't tingling, and I wasn't especially hungry. That is, not until now.

"Yeah," I said, nodding at nothing in particular. I looked around the kitchen of his parents' house. Porcelain gleamed like polished marble. Sunlight sifted through lace curtains. The checkered tile vibrated slightly. *Today is the first day of the rest of your life,* read a needlepoint hanging next to the Kanters' refrigerator. My senses felt so fresh and receptive that the sentiment rang true.

Greg took the bowl from my hands, adjusted a burner. A pat of butter hissed and skidded across the surface of the pan. Greg tilted the mixing bowl and down poured a braid of liquid egg. His body gently swayed as he stirred, face flushed from the heat. When he pulled two plates from a high shelf, the shirtsleeve slid down his arm and exposed the rise of his biceps. The odor of eggs made my stomach grumble.

One of the last holdouts in my high school, I'd never tried

marijuana. Greg was a veteran pot smoker — his sister, Jackie, always had a stash on hand — and since we had nothing to do that afternoon, he asked if he could "turn me on."

"Will I hallucinate?" I'd asked, trying to hide my apprehension. He locked the door to his room and threw open every window so his mother wouldn't smell the smoke.

"Maybe you'll look at your legs and, like, won't know they're yours for a second. Is that a hallucination?" In the time it took me to ponder this question, Greg lit a joint and thrust it into my hand. He told me how to hold it and inhale. "Blow the smoke out the window," he'd said. "If you need me, I'll be right here."

Half an hour later, we were setting our plates at the dining room table and eating scrambled eggs in silence. Relative silence. The grinding and suction of my own chewing, intensified by a dry mouth, echoed inside my head, a factory of mastication. I knew in a flash that this was happening to Greg, too, and we could barely look at each other for fear of erupting with laughter. "Maintain," Greg whispered before he choked on a bite of egg. He began to cough, his curly hair bobbing like a black chrysanthemum. "What's wrong, darling?" Mrs. Kanter called from the living room. Her meditation group, six middle-aged housewives, were seated on an L-shaped sectional. They tended to gossip and drink peppermint tea for hours before they finally lowered themselves, joints cracking, onto pillows and settled into a tableau of composure, sinking inward and breathing as one.

"Nothing's wrong," Greg yelled back. "I'm just choking on eggs." He looked at me, concerned.

"That sounded really weird," I said.

We couldn't trust ourselves to act normal around Mrs. Kanter, so we decided to abandon our lunch and take refuge in Jackie's room. The older of the two Kanter children, Jackie required privacy; she lived in a converted two-car garage behind the Kanters' house. Greg led me out the kitchen door and into the small, sunlit yard. Paved in concrete, the yard was barren except for a few orange trees growing from a patch of grass, remnants of the groves that had once been plentiful in the San Fernando Valley. When Greg knocked on her sliding-glass door, Jackie drew back the curtain and warily peered outside. Relieved to see it was only us, she unlocked the door and pulled it open. Her room was cloudy with smoke and ripe with the smell of marijuana. Sitar music wobbled and spun in circles. Greg threw his arm around me the moment we walked inside. "I got him stoned," he announced to his sister. Her smile dawned in slow motion. "That's beautiful," she said, beaming at me through gold-rimmed glasses. "Yeah," I said, taking note that this exclamation had replaced my entire vocabulary. Jackie rolled another joint — her tight joints were the envy of every pothead at our high school — and licked the gummed end of the cigarette paper with a single, expert pass of her tongue.

Greg and I walked around the room as though touring a museum. Tacked on the wall were posters whose phrases — EXPAND YOUR MIND, FLOWER POWER — were printed in psychedelic letters that seemed to bulge and melt beyond meaning. While Greg's room still contained the bunk beds and maple desk of his youth, Jackie's room consisted of castoffs: a tattered chair, a huge wooden spool that she used as a table, and a queen-size mattress on the floor, piled with clothes and records and books. In the far corner of the room stood a cage in which Thelonius, her rhesus monkey, feinted and bobbed like a tiny prizefighter. If anyone but Jackie approached him, Thelonius shrieked and bared his teeth, frantically swinging his hairy hands as if he were trying to toss them off his arms.

Jackie had acquired Thelonius from a local pet store a few weeks earlier, and only after a campaign of constant wheedling; her parents were opposed to the idea of a wild animal living in their daughter's room. Every time I'd visited the Kanters' house,

I heard her plead in a little-girl voice, "Please, can I have a monkey? He'd be so cute and I'll take really good care of him. Please, can I?" Then she would chatter and scratch her armpits, laughing her deep, delirious laugh. It's a miracle that Mr. and Mrs. Kanter never knew their daughter was stoned.

The three of us sat cross-legged on the floor and Jackie lit a fresh joint. "Yummy," she rasped, squinting against the smoke. Greg took a drag and his chest expanded. He sat perfectly still until a seed popped and a spark swam off the tip of the joint. Then he blinked and breathed and passed the joint to me. I took a slow toke. Greg and Jackie leaned forward, hands in their laps, their expressions protective and parental except for the fact that their eyes were glassy, their smiles beatific. The sitar music had stopped who knew how long ago and the needle skipped in the last groove, a susurration like steady rain. Holding the dope in my lungs, pressure built behind my eyes. Once I let go, a small fraction of the smoke I inhaled wafted out.

While we passed the joint, Thelonius chattered and gripped the bars of his cage. He stared at us as if pleading for release. I could barely look at his needy pink face. Still, it would have been worse had Jackie let him out. Paroled from his cage, Thelonius ricocheted around the room, yanking people's hair and hanging from their clothes, his fists pinching like vices. If he snatched a pair of sunglasses, keys, or cigarettes, only Jackie could coax him to let go, and not before a tug-of-war.

Once we finished the joint — the roach was placed in an ivory box along with several others — Jackie passed me a goatskin filled with cranberry juice. The sweet cool stream shot straight to my brain, radiating red. In the dim light, a vinyl miniskirt on Jackie's bed glinted like a shard of glass. Whorls in the wooden table looked as familiar as faces. Jackie put on Jimi Hendrix; electric guitar throbbed deep in my bones, and I felt as if my body were carved out of sound. When I offered him a drink,

Greg nodded yes and bobbed to the drumbeat. He tipped back his head, opened his mouth, and squeezed the goatskin.

I liked being high. Anything could happen.

*

Which was exactly what frightened me about the prospect of smoking marijuana in the first place. Wouldn't it loosen the bolts of inhibition? What if I grabbed my friend and kissed him?

Greg and I had been inseparable throughout the eleventh grade. We routinely tested the parameters of friendship, trying to see how much we could merge and still be ourselves. We lent each other clothes, talked on the telephone twice a night, and helped each other cram for tests. We knew that friendships as intense and intimate as ours were more common among females, but Greg and I were hippies who scoffed at rigid definitions, seeking all that was strange and amorphous in human nature, amused when someone momentarily mistook us for girls because of our long hair. Among our circle of friends — girls wearing pants and combat boots, boys wearing beads and flowered shirts — manhood and womanhood were concepts in quotes, words that conjured thick-necked jocks and beauty queens. The institution of marriage and the rituals of dating seemed to us as outmoded as a prom or a hayride, the corny, bourgeois inventions of an older generation. When it came to our roles as young men and women, we dressed and behaved against expectations, and socialized in a loving clump.

Greg and I relished the inappropriate and prided ourselves on our ability to turn mischief into art. We sneaked off campus for lunch and, after scarfing down a couple of Jack in the Box burgers, drove backward past the drive-thru, speaking in reverse and handing our empty bags back to the man at the window. Sure, he was annoyed at first, but soon Jack — or so we called him — was posing for lunchtime snapshots with the rest of our friends who ditched school in order to try the same trick; he seemed glad for the distraction and his celebrity among a bunch of hungry kids.

Even when we were alone, Greg and I never thought much about the way we were *supposed* to behave. Sometimes I'd drill him for our weekly vocabulary quiz while he took a bath, a study habit his parents might have thought peculiar had they known. The words I asked him to define — *lachrymose, myriad, corporeal, bovine* — resounded off the tile walls. Over the top of the notebook I could see his chest and arms, and when he turned to find the soap, the muscled breadth of his back. The hair on his haunches, his wrinkled penis stirred by currents of bath water — the sight of him naked drenched my senses, and no vocabulary was large enough to describe the effect it had on me. I stared without staring, a feat like the one-handed clapping his mother had told us about. The air we breathed was hot and humid, and I had to wipe my forehead again and again as I went down the list of definitions. The mirror and the window fogged. Drops of water beaded on the walls and, no longer able to contain their own weight, fell in glittering rivulets. I was flooded with longing, a longing that went back as far as I could remember and grew more abundant the longer I lived, brimming in that room with Greg.

We were two seventeen-year-old boys who had recently discovered our vanity, which was a little like discovering a crater in one's backyard; our need for attention was startling and deep. Greg and I spent whole afternoons rummaging through racks of used clothes at thrift stores, talking each other into and out of faded bell-bottoms and monogrammed bowling shirts. "Groovy," we'd say. Or "Gross." It was during one of these shopping expeditions that we got into a discussion about male beauty; most men had difficulty admitting that they could appreciate other men physically, which we decided was a kind of cowardice, and not surprising given the fact that John Wayne, a mechanical cowboy, was an ideal of American manhood. "The guy's bovine," I said. "You bet," said Greg in a drawl like the Duke's. European men, Greg added, kissed one another on both cheeks when they greeted, and nobody made a fuss. Later that night, I replayed his remark and tried to find within it a glimmer of lust, a hidden invitation.

There was none. Greg was a boy who enjoyed the fluid shape of human affection; he could hug me all he wanted and it wouldn't alter the fact that he was heterosexual. On the other hand, gestures that were playful for Greg would have been for me a kind of admission, a commitment to be the queer I'd always suspected I was. If I acted on my urges I'd cross a line, and I worried there'd be no turning back. While I was the one who harbored desire, Greg was the more demonstrative. He was as close to a lover as I might ever have, for all I knew then, a boy who might even continue to be my friend if he found out the truth. Might. It was a tricky proposition. Even the most liberal and iconoclastic men were likely to be frightened by fags. Greg knew about Michelangelo, for example, but that didn't mean he'd feel comfortable taking a bath in front of him. For seventeen years I'd resorted to deceit if it meant risking a friendship. The more boundless my affection for Greg, the more precise my silence.

I grew heavy and restless with pent-up affection. I wanted to bridge the difference between us, wanted us to share an airtight bond. This was especially true when it came to Greg's mantra. Mrs. Kanter had encouraged him to take classes in meditation, which she believed could improve her son's powers of concentration and leave him fresh-headed for the future. Once he completed the preliminary phase of training — one day he showed me the lotus position, closed his eyes, and enlightened me to his extravagant lashes — Greg was ready to meet with his guru. For a small fee, he would receive his mantra along with a few dozen other disciples. One of the guru's wealthy followers had provided a private house for the occasion, and Greg was allowed to bring one friend.

He gripped the steering wheel of his mother's yellow Impala and explained, with waning patience, that certain sounds had contemplative properties and, if repeated, would help him reach a state of inner peace.

I asked, "Is it a sound or a word?"

"A meaningful sound," he said, "and a meaningless word."

I squinted at him. "Did you think of that just now?"

Greg smiled, inscrutable. I figured this was something his guru had told him and the thought of my friend's transcendental endeavor suddenly irked me. The car climbed into the hills above the Sunset Strip. The higher we went, the better the view, the more expensive the neighborhood. Above an endless band of smog, the sky was blinding, bluer than blue. There were no houses in sight, only wrought-iron gates and wide brick driveways hinted that people lived in these hills.

"How many mantras are there?" I asked.

He didn't know, and seemed to consider the quantity of mantras a petty detail.

"Does everybody get the same sound?"

"No," he said. "I think it's, like, an individual thing." He handed me the invitation and asked me to check the address.

He parked the car and we hiked up a steep driveway. A lone man sat in a patch of shade and strummed a zither. I could see from a distance that every door and window of the huge Spanish house had been flung open, and people drifted in and out. As we came closer, the murmur of voices seemed to arise from everywhere at once like the drone of bees. The guests wore Indian shirts, fringed shawls, and long dresses. Where, I wondered, was the owner? It could have been any one of a dozen people, given the way everyone made themselves at home: guests lolled on the front steps, plucked flowers, or lit sticks of incense. I couldn't tell the bystanders from those who had come to receive their mantra. Greg had brought a jar of honey wrapped in muslin as an offering, and though he wasn't sure where to leave it or where to go to meet his guru, he refused to ask anyone for advice, preferring instead to carry the jar with him while he mingled and nodded and talked to strangers.

I lost track of him in no time and wandered through the sparsely furnished house, blinded by the white walls and sunlight glaring off wooden floors. After I stopped to listen to a little boy pounding the keys of a grand piano, I drifted outside and explored the backyard. Narrow terraces rose up the side of the mountain, a labyrinth of vegetable gardens and flower beds and weathered arbors. Along the way I passed couples who were holding hands. One pair stared into each other's eyes and probed each other's faces with their fingers, as if sculpting busts from lumps of clay. Seen from the back, a few of the couples looked like pairs of women or pairs of long-haired men. I wished I could find Greg and thought how much I missed being with him, a longing I quickly dismissed. Even in a world as loose and accepting and sensuous as this, desire like mine seemed out of place.

Greg finally found me sitting on the rim of a shallow pond behind the house, watching fish dart back and forth while I listened to wind chimes. He came up from behind and tapped me on the shoulder. I wanted to ask him where he'd been, wanted to scold him for leaving me alone, but I couldn't betray my possessiveness, not in so pacific a setting. I said hello as though I hadn't missed him, acting as if I could barely tear my attention away from the fish. He didn't have the honey, so I thought he'd probably gotten his mantra. I didn't ask him. Not right away.

"Do you like it?" I ventured as we drove down the mountain.

"Sure," he said. "But liking or not liking your mantra isn't the point."

"Is it complicated? To remember, I mean."

"Not especially. Using it correctly is the hard part."

We descended into a layer of smog, and the light took on a yellow cast. Greg fiddled with the radio.

"Do you feel any different now that you have it?"

What a relief to hear him say no.

"Tell me your mantra," I said point-blank.

Greg laughed. "I can't tell you my mantra."

"Why not?"

"It's something I say to myself, not something I say out loud."

A word sat inside him, and I had to have it. "Is it *antidisestablishmentarianism?*"

He snorted and shook his head.

"*Rumpelstiltskin?*"

"Stop," he said. He punched buttons, and the radio sputtered.

The prospect of his inner journey filled me with panic; in order to find enlightenment, he'd leave me behind.

"Don't you trust me?"

"Of course I trust . . ."

"Oh please, can I have your mantra," I said, imitating Jackie's plea for a monkey. "I'll take really good care of it. Please, can I?" I thought this would make him laugh, would soften him up and cause him to give in.

He turned off the radio. "You're bumming me," he warned.

"Is it *evanescent? Pantaloons?*"

Greg gripped the wheel and stared at the road.

"OK," I conceded. "My lips are sealed." But language still took shape in my head. While Greg nursed a single word, I churned with guesswork and speculation. In any case, the rest of the drive was quiet.

*

A few weeks later we were getting high together for the first time, an experience I could chalk up as one more thing I shared with Greg. My attempt to rob him of his mantra had been all but forgotten. The Beatles' "A Day in the Life" was playing on the stereo. Jackie turned up the volume. She asked me to close my eyes and concentrate on the crescendo in which the London Philharmonic plays every instrument at once, a chord that builds in pressure and pitch. I'd heard the song several times before, but now the final note droned on and on. I opened my eyes, stranded in sound. Old pros at aural hallucination, Greg and Jackie had anticipated my reaction. Greg shouted that the same thing had happened to him. "Isn't it incredible?" he asked. "It just keeps stretching."

"And stretching," I echoed. The two of us cocked our heads to listen, and Jackie glanced back and forth between us.

"You really love my brother," she shouted a second after the crescendo ended. Her words rang out, a sonic boom. She was staring straight at me, and I tried to smile.

Before I knew it, the subject had changed. "What flavor do you guys want next," she asked, thumbing through a stack of records, "Strawberry Alarm Clock or Vanilla Fudge?" Greg waved a hand in front of his face. "I'm streaking," he said. Thelonius chattered and sucked on a walnut.

The taboo seemed tame once it had been uttered, one small wave in a stream of sensation. So what if I loved her brother; the very idea seemed to make Jackie happy. As far as she was concerned, Greg and I were proof of harmony among mankind. And Greg didn't bat an extravagant eyelash; a moment later, he asked if I wanted to stay overnight. I began to relax, to "go with the flow," as Jackie would have said. I let out a sigh, closed my eyes, and drifted through the music.

*

That night, after the effects of the marijuana had worn off, I felt as if I'd returned to the Kanters' house from a foreign country.

Greg and I were sprawled on the floor of his room doing our English homework. I read Dylan Thomas's poem about "the force that through the green fuse drives the flower," its sound and sense inseparable. Greg and I had washed the dishes and put away leftovers, but the smell of Mr. Kanter's vegetarian lasagna still permeated the house. The window was open, and I could see that the light was on in Jackie's room, her curtain rippling in the wind that swept through the valley and shook the leaves of orange trees. Every now and then, the sound of applause wafted from her television set. Closing my book, I savored the scene with the weary gratitude of a traveler.

When we decided to call it a night, Greg paced around his room while he brushed his teeth. Posing with a foamy grin, he tried to make a joke about having rabies without spitting toothpaste onto his clothes or the carpet. I slipped into the lower bunk and zipped up his ancient sleeping bag. The flannel lining felt soft against my skin and smelled like a tired boy in the wilderness. Greg had gone to the bathroom to rinse out his mouth, and after he came back, he ground his clean teeth to show me how they squeaked. The sound gave me gooseflesh. He climbed the ladder at the side of the bed and wrestled with his clothes in the bunk above me. Jeans and socks and underwear rained onto the floor below. Maybe it was an aftereffect of the marijuana, but I lay on my back and stared up through the bottom of his mattress as if I had X-ray vision. The stiff denim would leave pink creases in his hips. He'd rub his feet when the socks were peeled off, and smell the T-shirt before he tossed it, his collarbone shining in the overhead light. Even at a distance, even out of sight, his body seemed close and palpable, a geography I could imagine at will.

Greg turned out the lights and we said good night. Slowly the room emerged from the dark. And still I saw him hover above me. The need to touch him rushed through my fingers, heedless as blood. I thought of the times I'd hugged my pillow. Or grazed other boys in the name of play and committed their skin to memory. Or kissed my own arm, then tried to divide myself and feel the force of another's ardor. And where had all this fantasy gotten me? In a bottom bunk, wide awake, cinched within the limits of my body.

I heard the bed creak, saw legs dangle in the air above me, feet poised for the floor. Greg sat on the edge of the upper bunk, about to jump down to get a drink of water or go to the bathroom. A pause as he yawned. I'm not sure where my plan came from, but it occurred to me unbidden, so swift and simple that I had to act. I could always blame my audacity on the marijuana. I could say I woke up, thought he was falling, and then lurched out of bed to catch him. I could say I was just obeying instinct. And that, after all, was the truth.

In an instant I convinced myself that if my plan failed, Greg would simply fall through my arms — no anger, shock, or consequence — and quietly leave the room. But the fact is I grabbed him the second he landed. He spun around in the cage of my embrace. His hipbones were blunt, his pubic hair coarse, his navel inches away from my face. That I'd gone this far seemed impossible. I could smell his body's privacy, a distillation of sweat and sex, and it hit me like a whiff of ether, like something I dreamed I breathed. My muscles shuddered. My hands were flat against the small of his back, too disembodied to feel his flesh.

He gripped my arms tightly, as if he were going to push them away, though he didn't let go. For a second, I thought my fears had been foolish. For a second, I thought he might yield without a protest. For a second I wasn't sorry.

Still, I didn't know what to do with him next. Fantasy was one thing, its kisses leading seamlessly to further kisses. But finally holding a man in my hands gave me only an incredulous, guilty pleasure, like holding stolen money. It's not that I didn't want him, or doubted my desire; it was as though I had waited too long, had anticipated this moment too fervently and often, and now I could only sit there and tell myself this was actually happening, so stunned by the gulf between fantasy and fact that I couldn't give in to abandon.

"I can't," he said, finally prying open my arms and pulling away. "It's . . . I don't have it in me. I don't feel those things. Not as much as you do. Maybe it's society or something. Maybe you're braver than I am." He backed away — his naked body lost definition with every sentence, with every step — and fled to get a drink of water.

I sat on the lower bunk as if in the recess of a drawer, so vacant of love or regret or alarm, the wind might as well have been moving through me. I could hear it sift though the window screen and scour the walls of the Kanters' house.

*

Six years after that night I will have lost contact with Greg Kanter altogether, hearing secondhand of his marriage to a social worker, his two sons, his life on the East Coast. Six years after that night my home was a bachelor apartment in Hollywood, a crumbling Mediterranean building that had once been owned by a silent film star. I was free to go out and meet a man, though I hadn't been able to leave my narrow quarters and translate this idea into action. One of my walls was adjacent to a staircase, and all night I heard my neighbors come and go as I finished my graduate work — papers about abstract expressionism and conceptual art — their footsteps a constant reproach.

When I finally mustered the courage to bring a man back to my apartment, I closed the door behind us and my home seemed small, a cloister or cocoon. Jacob was older, bearded. I'd chosen him because his face was thoughtful and kind, because his green gaze didn't leave room for doubt, and because his body looked strong and compact. I offered him something to drink and we talked about the place we'd met that night, a bar whose interior was fashioned after a city street, storefronts lining the walls, stars painted upon the ceiling, a world turned inside out. While we talked, Jacob browsed through my bookshelf and pulled out *Language, Thought and Reality,* by Benjamin Whorf. There were other books on linguistics — Wittgenstein, Chomsky — required reading for a class I never took. "Do you understand semantics?" he asked. I admitted that I'd never read the books and joked about how they were meant to impress my dates. The second I did this, I imploded with loneliness. He turned the book over and read from the jacket: "The structure of a person's language is a factor in the way in which he understands reality and behaves with respect to it . . ."

I interrupted and told him I'd never been with a man before. He slipped the book back on the shelf. "We don't have to do anything," he said. "We can just talk."

My mattress sat in an alcove where a Murphy bed had once folded down from the wall, and I maneuvered him toward it while we kissed and shed our clothes. His purple shirt split open in my hands like the skin of an overripe plum. His beard smelled musky and elemental. Yes, I said at the pressure of his flesh. I entered him eagerly — he guided me with his hands — and by entering his body that night I pushed through the skin of another life.

*

But for now I'm in Greg's room, huddled in a bunk. He returned with a glass of water, unable or unwilling to acknowledge that something momentous had happened, that things between us would never be the same. "We can still be friends," he said, climbing up the ladder. "We don't have to mention this ever again."

I slipped back into the sleeping bag. I heard him pounding his pillow above me, tossing and turning till he finally fell asleep. Outside, the wind pushed its way everywhere, touched everything at once. I watched Jackie's window across the dark yard. She'd let Thelonious out of his cage, and his restless shadow was cast against the curtain. He leapt about, clung to what he could, his distant chatter almost like language.

Truth Serum

~~~~~~~~~~~~~~~~~~~~~~~~~~~~~~

Every Tuesday at exactly three o'clock, the nurse would call my name and lead me into the examining room, where I lay down on a padded table. Comfortable? she always asked, and always I said yes without conviction. I have no recollection of the woman's face, only her white, immaculate back, and the click of the door as it closed behind her. I'd be counting holes in the soundproof ceiling when Dr. Sward, my psychotherapist, would bound into the room. The man possessed an inexhaustible energy when it came to the task of psychological exploration, and I think he hoped some of his enthusiasm would rub off on his reticent clients. Dr. Sward prided himself on being a hale, contented fellow, a man able to overcome adversity. A former smoker, he'd had an operation to remove part of his larynx, and his voice, or what remained of it, was somnolent and gravelly. "Hello," he'd rasp. "Are we ready?" Dr. Sward took a seat in the room's only chair — vinyl exhaled under his weight — and removed a fountain pen and note pad from the breast pocket of his blazer. Pen poised, he beamed a broad and expectant grin, a lock of white hair falling onto his forehead.

Next would enter Dr. Townsley, Dr. Sward's stout, mustachioed colleague, who swabbed my arm with alcohol and asked me to make a fist. I barely felt the injection, but serum rode into my vein like an intravenous hot toddy, and a primal comfort seemed to radiate outward from the tip of the needle. Almost instantly, I began to take in rich, intoxicating breaths of air. I steeped in a heedless stew of sensation: felt the rubber release from my arm; heard small talk volley between the doctors; saw shiny fronds of a philodendron, which seemed like the greenest things on earth. With the sudden candor of a drunk, I wanted to tell the doctors how happy I felt, but before the words could form, I heard the sound of what I thought was a receptionist typing in another room. Her typing would quicken — faster, manic, superhuman — and invariably I would think to myself: A million words per minute! What nimble fingers! The keys must be shooting sparks from friction! And then I'd realize it wasn't the sound of typing after all, but something more miraculous — chattering watts of light showered down from a bulb on the ceiling. Stirred to the verge of tears, I wanted to shout, "Hold everything, doctors. I can hear light!" But my jaw went lax and my fist unclenched and I lost my grip on consciousness.

When I opened my eyes, the overhead lights were out. Dr. Townsley had gone, and Dr. Sward's voice emanated from somewhere near the wan glow of a table lamp. "How are you?" he asked.

I was eager to answer any question. I effervesced with things to say. I couldn't have lifted my head if I'd wanted to. "Good," I mumbled, trying to work the moisture back into my mouth. "Very good."

Dr. Sward believed that this experimental form of therapy would help me get to the root of my problem. It was 1974, and his colleagues were having some success with the treatment, a combination of sodium pentothol, known during the Second World War as "truth serum," and Ritalin, a mild amphetamine that helps hyperactive children gather their scattered thoughts. The sodium pentothol, he'd explained, would cause me to pass out, and the Ritalin would revive me. This paradoxical cocktail was supposed to numb a patient's inhibitions while at the same time enhancing his capacity for insight. Its effect vanished without a trace in about forty minutes. Dr. Sward suggested the drugs after I told him that talking to him for the past six months had done nothing to reduce the frequency or intensity of my sexual fantasies involving men. *Frequency, intensity,* these were the terms we used, as though the clinical distance they imposed was in itself an achievement, a way of dividing me from the heat and draw of desire. The final decision was up to me; no treatment could make me change if I didn't have a strong desire to do so, but I might, he felt, be resistant, and the drugs could break down my unconscious defenses and hasten our progress.

"How are things at home?" asked Dr. Sward.

I'd been living with a woman for three years, a woman whom I loved, and with whom I had a sex life both playful and pleasurable. I met Bia at the California Institute of the Arts in 1970. Passing her dorm room, I'd watch her cut bits of black-and-white photographs out of *Time* magazine with an X-Acto blade and then paste the fragments into long, hieroglyphic columns, giving current events a cryptic twist. In a circle of lamplight, she worked with the meticulous intensity of a jeweler, her concentration unaffected by the jazz blaring from her stereo. We began to eat dinner together at a local restaurant called the Happy Steak, and it was there, amid the faux cowhide upholstery and Formica wood-grain tables, that we honed our love of the lowbrow, discussing at length the soup cans and crushed cars of contemporary art. Budding conceptualists, we were indifferent to the *taste* of the steak but delighted by the *idea* that our dinners were impaled with a plastic cow, its flank branded RARE, MEDIUM, or WELL. Instead of saying grace before we ate, we'd bow our heads, clasp our hands, and recite, "Cows are happy when they cry / So we kick them in the eye."

I'm not sure at what point friendship turned to love — our relationship remained platonic for nearly a year — but I'm sure we would have had sex much earlier if both of us hadn't harbored longings for people of the same gender. My secret crushes included Robert Conrad, whose television show, "The Wild Wild West," had him stripped to the waist in almost every episode, his pectorals a lesson in advanced geometry, and Bill Medley of the Righteous Brothers, with whom I'd been smitten since junior high, romanticizing into satyrhood his long, lean, horsey face. Bia, it turned out, was crazy for Greta Garbo, piqued by her high cheekbones, moist eyes, and the world-weary manner that suggested a womanhood rich in glamorous disappointments. We confided these guilty attractions late one night during a marathon conversation. Once they were aired, our admissions seemed less shameful, less significant, and I began to feel that sleeping with Bia was inevitable; who better to sleep with than the keeper of your secrets? Besides, as a side effect of our heated discussions, her translucent skin and hazel eyes had begun to excite me.

The only word to describe our first sexual encounter is *premeditated*. We gave ourselves weeks to get used to the idea of sleeping together, to weigh the consequences (would physical intimacy jeopardize our friendship?), to prolong the delicious anticipation. Like a couple catering a large party, we tried to take into account every eventuality, every shift in the weather, every whim of appetite. Hers was the bed we'd use; it was the biggest, the most familiar; we'd sat on it for countless hours, smoking Marlboros, listening to jazz, watching TV with the sound turned down while improvising snappy patter. Intercourse, we decided, would be best in the late afternoon when the window shades turned Bia's room the color of butter. Afterward we'd shower together, and have a meal at the Happy Steak.

When the day we'd set aside finally arrived, we spent the morning walking through Descanso Gardens. Arms about each other, we were tender and nervous and telepathic, taking this path instead of that, staring at schools of darting koi, lingering before stands of cactus, awed by their bright, incongruous blossoms.

*

I had slept with only one person up to that point, a girl with whom I'd gone to high school. Alison would whip her long blond hair from side to side, a semaphore of the feminine. Her arms and legs were hard and tan, and she seemed, walking to class or sprawled on the lawn, all loose-limbed and eager, a living invitation. Alison loved sex. Got it as often and with as many boys as she could. Her flirtations had about them an ingenuous joy, a stark curiosity. The sexual revolution was in full swing, and Alison's hedonism gave her a certain cachet.

The night before I left for college on the East Coast, I took her to a bar on the top floor of a high-rise in Hollywood. We shared fierce and slippery kisses in the elevator. Toasting each other at a tiny table, the city glittered below us. Men looked at her with lust and at me with envy; her company quelled my sexual doubts. I knew we wouldn't sleep together that night — she had to drive back home to Malibu before her parents returned from a trip — and this knowledge freed me from the performance anxiety that surely would have swamped me had sex been imminent. I helped her off with her coat, toyed with her hair, and paid the bill, playing my masculine role to the hilt because I knew there was no pressure to follow through. I'd carry with me to college the memory of our date, a talisman to ward off the fear that I might never escape my desire for men.

Imagine my surprise when, two months later, Alison showed up at my Brooklyn dormitory wearing a skimpy white dress in the middle of winter, an overnight bag slung over her shoulder. We hadn't seen or written to each other since our date. She'd been visiting her cousins on Long Island and wanted to surprise me. "You're hilarious," she said when I suggested she stay in the guest room at the end of the hallway. She flopped onto my bed. Kicked off her shoes. Fixed me in her bright green gaze. Flipped her hair to and fro like a flag.

We batted her overnight bag off the bed and it skidded across the floor. Articles of clothing arced through the air. I tried, with brusque adjustments of my hips, to disguise any tentativeness when I entered her. It's now or never, I remember thinking. Her vagina was silky, warm, and capacious. It struck me that my penis might be too small to fill her in the way she wanted, and just when I thought that this tightening knot of self-consciousness might make the act impossible, she let out a yelp of unabashed pleasure. I plunged in deeper, single-minded as a salmon swimming upstream. My hands swept the slope of Alison's shoulders, the rise of her breasts. I didn't realize it until afterward, but I sucked her neck the entire time, fastened by my lips to a bucking girl. Alison's climax was so protracted, her moans so operatic, her nails so sharp as they raked my back, that when she sat up and felt her neck, I thought she was checking her pulse. Suddenly, she rose and ran to the bathroom, a swath of bed sheet trailing in her wake. "I told you," she shrieked, her voice resounding off the tile walls. She appeared in the doorway, legs in a wide, defiant stance, nipples erect. "I told you no hickeys!"

"No you didn't."

"I said it right at the beginning."

"Then I didn't hear you, Alison."

She held her hand to her neck, Cleopatra bitten by an asp. "What am I going to do?" Her voice was about to break. "What am I going to tell my cousins?"

It was preposterous; she had come to Brooklyn to seduce me, and now Alison was mortified by the small, sanguine badge of our abandon. I said I was sorry.

"'Sorry' isn't going to take it away."

"What about this," I said, turning to show her the marks I could feel scored into my back.

"Oh, great," she said. "Let's compare war wounds." She bent down and scooped up her white dress; it lay on the floor like a monstrous corsage. "You men," she said bitterly.

Forgive me, I was flattered. Placed at last in a class from which I'd felt barred.

I lit a cigarette, watching as she stood before the window and dragged a brush through her hair, the strokes punishing, relentless, and I began to see that Alison was angry at herself for the rapacious nature of her needs, and that her future, overpopulated with lonely men, would be one long, unresolved argument between ardor and regret. Or was I seeing my own fate in her?

An icy sky dimmed above the city. Alison shook her head at an offer of dinner. Her face, framed by sheaths of yellow hair, was pinched with the reflex to flee. "So," she sighed. She slipped into her shoes, stared through me and toward the door. "Give me a call someday." Her tone was clipped and bitter. Standing in my bathrobe, at a loss for what to say, I touched her shoulder and she shrugged me away, managing a weak and fleeting smile before she shut the door behind her.

When I turned around, I saw that night veiled the Brooklyn skyline. I tried not to think how far I was from home. Touching was futile; men or women, what did it matter? I crawled back into bed — the residue of Alison's odor rose from the pillow like a puff of dust — and fell into a dreamless sleep.

*

It would be a long time before I had sex again. I told myself, with a sad resolve, that lovemaking was not one of my natural skills; all mixed-up when it came to desire, I'd have to depend on something other than sex for satisfaction. Somewhere I'd read that

Picasso spent a lifetime channeling his libido into painting (this explained his prodigious output), and I secretly hoped that my erotic energy would be sublimated into art. Deprivation for the sake of art — the idea made me feel noble. It's no coincidence that during this period my class projects became huge and ornate, and although I hadn't the slightest understanding of, say, the mathematical principles behind my three-dimensional model of the Golden Rectangle, my efforts were often singled out for discussion by instructors impressed with the obsessive detail that had begun to characterize my work. One night, after too much to drink, this obsessiveness led me to paint my dorm room cobalt blue and glue dozens of Styrofoam cups to the ceiling, thinking they looked like stalactites. It took three coats of white latex to rectify the situation. Woozy from fumes, I began to understand sublimation's wild, excessive underside. Soon after that night, restless and homesick, I transferred to art school in California, where I met Bia.

Bia was still a virgin when we made our plans to sleep together, a fact I took into account when I clipped my toenails, conditioned my pubic hair with cream rinse, and practically baptized myself with Brut before I walked into her room. My ablutions were not in vain; our sex was greedy, sweet-smelling teamwork. Spent as we were in the aftermath, we radiated fresh contentment. I rested my head on Bia's breast, grateful for my good luck and the buttery light. That afternoon we began to live together; devotion, a knot we'd tied with our bodies.

As for our homosexual yearnings, once we became a couple, we didn't bring them up again out of affection and deference; like the foundation of a house, they remained present but unseen; the trust that prompted such confidences was the basis of our relationship. Both of us, I think, wanted to believe that we were embarking on the grand adventure of heterosexuality, and that the fear of ostracism with which we had lived for so much of our lives could be shucked off at last like a pair of tight shoes. We were relieved, those first few years of living together, to see our love reflected back at us from movies and billboards and books. Never taking for granted the privilege of public touching, we kissed in cars and markets and parks. But there persisted for me this unavoidable fact: regardless of how gratifying I found sex with Bia, I wanted to have a man.

*

"Knock, knock. Is anybody there?" joked Dr. Sward. "I was asking what's new."

In the first few seconds of every session, consciousness was something I tried on for size like a huge droopy hat. Then I'd blurt a forbidden thought. "The Armenian who works the steampress machine at the dry cleaners was wearing a T-shirt, and I swear I could feel the fur on his forearms from across the room." Usually Dr. Sward greeted my disclosures with a bromide. Once I told him that every masturbatory fantasy I'd ever had involved a man, and that I'd gotten to the point where I frankly didn't see how psychotherapy, no matter how probing, enhanced by drugs or not, could alter an impulse etched into my brain by years of unrelenting lust. Dr. Sward laughed his hearty laugh. I thought I heard him lean forward in his chair. He suggested I substitute the image of a woman for the image of a man the second before I ejaculated. I considered telling him that if I had to concentrate on his advice I'd never be able to come, but his casual tone made change seem so easy, like using a giant vaudeville hook to yank an awful act off the stage.

Despite the fact that his advice was often facile, I continued to visit Dr. Sward once a week. He was sincere in his efforts to change me; I was the ambivalent party, tired of grappling with secret lust, yet riveted by the bodies of men. I blamed myself for the inability to reform, chalked it up to a failure of will, and would have tried just about anything that promised relief from confusion and shame. Determined to spend my life with Bia — she was my ally in art; there was no one with whom I had more fun — I thought it might be worth enduring my frustrations with therapy in order to ensure the longevity of our relationship. Perhaps there would come a point where my sexual impulses would be simplified, a straight line where there once had been all the twists and turns of a French curve. I knew few gay men, and to some extent still believed that homosexuals were doomed to a life of unhappiness; I hadn't entirely exorcised the images of homosexuality that figured into the rumors and hearsay of my childhood, images of gloomy, clandestine encounters, with trench coats and candy as the recurrent motifs. I suppose I understood that no behavioral modification, no psychological revelation, was going to take away my desire for men, but in the end I went back to Dr. Sward's office because — this is the hardest confession of all — because I wanted to hear the light.

The terrible power of that sound. When I tried to describe it to Bia, I resorted to the phrase *the music of the spheres.* How lazy and inadequate! The universe seemed to be shuddering, seized by a vast, empathic spasm, crying out in a tremulous voice. I don't mean only visible stuff — chairs and cars and buildings and trees — but microcosmic tremblings, too — pollen and protons and cosmic dust. The sum of matter was like a tuning fork that had been struck, and one vital, cacophonous chord issued from a light bulb screwed into the ceiling of a room where I lay on a padded table and tried to revise my life. Compared to that sound, all the doctor's concern, all my apprehension, all the rules governing who touches whom, were muffled to a feeble squeak. The glory of it left me breathless.

Now I would never claim that the sound was a panacea, but it became an extremely beneficial aspect of therapy, given the way it trivialized my problems with its big aural blast. Dr. Sward believed that my desire for men could be broken down into a set of constituent griefs: lack of paternal love; envy toward other men for their sexual certainty; a need for identification confused with a drive for physical contact. And then, one day, the blare of the light still ringing in my ears, I asked the doctor if heterosexual desire wasn't also a muddled, complex matter, fraught with the very same helplessness and hurt he attributed to my particular case. Didn't he, for example, ever seek his wife's maternal attentions, or envy her sexual receptivity, or yearn to burrow into her flesh, his nerves alert and bordering on anguish? Without a dose of desperation, or the aches and pains left over from one's past, what would sex between two people be? A pat on the back?

All the things I believed to be true pushed from behind like a harried crowd; it was the sodium pentothol talking. The silence that followed embarrassed us both. Worried that my challenge to his authority had upset him, I backpedaled a bit. "I'm just thinking out loud, you know, trying to fit the pieces together."

"Of course," said Dr. Sward. "Of course. But after all, we're not here to talk about me."

*

I saw Dr. Sward for another six months before I announced, emboldened by an especially heady dose of serum, that I felt it was time for me to terminate therapy. He offered no argument. In fact, he was surprisingly willing to see me leave, and I couldn't help but think my visits had become for him a source of professional, if not personal, disappointment. For the past year Dr. Sward had insisted that because I lived with a woman and enjoyed with her a passionate sex life, I was, *ipso facto*, heterosexual — a conclusion which struck me as absurd, like thinking that, when Charles Laughton played Henry VIII, he was actually the king of England. During our final sessions, however, Dr. Sward seemed resigned to my conflict, more respectful of the obstinate, wayward power of human want.

"Would you say," he asked rather pensively at the end of our last session, "that the nature of your homosexual fantasies has changed at all during the course of our working together?"

"They've changed a little," I said to placate him. I meant that they occurred with even greater frequency.

"Will you attempt a hetero- or homosexual life after you leave this office?"

"Don't know," I lied, sliding off the table and shaking his hand. We sighed and wished each other luck.

What I did know was that, as far as the outcome of sodium pentothol therapy was concerned, the one truth that mattered to me now was the electrifying strength of lust. Still, I made no effort to leave Bia for months after I quit seeing Dr. Sward. I was frightened of uncertainty, of exile to a shapeless fate, and the closer I came to a life without her, the more her company soothed me.

When I finally did tell her I wanted to move out and test my feelings for men, we were sitting side by side at Kennedy Airport, waiting to board a plane back to Los Angeles after a vacation in New York City. Destinations echoed over the loudspeaker. Travelers checked their boarding passes, gathered at gates. All that rush and flux, all those strangers embarking on journeys, made urgent and keen my sense of departure. I turned to Bia and, before I knew what I was doing, mumbled that there was something I had to say. I kept protesting my affection, my helplessness. I wanted desperately to take her hand, to hold her to me, but fought it down as a hypocritical impulse. She stared at me, uncomprehending, as though I were pleading in a foreign language. Then the dawning of fury and hurt as she understood.

Once on the plane, our steady, defeated weeping was disguised by the roar of the engines. Every time I turned to face her, at a loss for what to say, I glimpsed our reflections in the airplane window, vague and straying above the earth.

It wasn't until long after I'd moved out, after Bia found a woman and I found a man, that I mustered the courage to tell her what had happened in New York. We'd spent the afternoon at opposite ends of Manhattan, she uptown, having lunch with a friend, and me in SoHo, visiting galleries. Walking back to our midtown hotel, I cut through the West Village. It was hot and humid and overcast, the dark air charged with impending rain. Men congregated on the sidewalk or shared tables at outdoor cafés, their sleeves rolled up, shirts unbuttoned, talk and gestures intent. A few of them turned to watch me pass. Self-conscious, I actually believed for a moment that they were straight men who thought I was gay, and I regretted wearing the gauzy Indian shirt I'd bought at an import shop and that now felt as insubstantial as lingerie. I began to walk faster, as though I might outstrip the realization of what and where I was.

A salvo of thunder, a blanching flash of light, and there began a heavy, tepid rain. People ran for cover in doorways, gathered under awnings drummed by the rain. My shirt was drenched in seconds, patches of my bare skin seeping through the fabric like stains. I kept tugging the cloth away from my body, but the wet shirt clung and flesh bloomed through. Dressed yet exposed in the middle of the city, arms folded across my chest, I froze as though in an anxious dream. Then I dashed into the nearest doorway where another man stood, waiting out the rain. He had a round, guileless face and brown hair beaded with drops of water. "You're positively soaked," he said. We eyed each other nervously, then peered up at the sluggish clouds. He was neither especially handsome nor especially interesting, but his small talk — he knew where I could buy an umbrella, hoped he had closed his apartment windows — calmed me. His weathered neck, encircled by a gold chain, made me wonder how old he was and if he spent long hours in the sun on a balcony somewhere in the city, with friends perhaps, or the man with whom he lived, and I glimpsed, as if through the window of his skin, a life more solid and settled than my own. He was, I decided, a man who'd adapted to his own desires; I envied him his sexual certainty, and thus bore out, although in reverse, one of Dr. Sward's theories. I would have had sex with that talkative, innocuous stranger in an instant, would have gladly given him the burden of releasing me from ambivalence. And just when it occurred to me that it might be possible to seduce him, just as I wrestled with a proposition, the rain let up, and he wished me luck and dashed down the street.

I walked aimlessly, for hours, till the pale sun made my shirt opaque.

That night, when Bia reached out in her sleep to touch me, she touched a man on the edge of action, shedding the skin of his former life. I tossed and turned. The hotel bed felt hard and unfamiliar. I didn't know then that Bia and I would remain life-long friends, or that by never again falling in love with someone of the opposite sex, we'd preserve the anomaly of who we once were. I knew only that impatience outweighed my remorse. Over and over, I replayed my encounter with the man in the doorway; in fantasy, I lived on my own, and when he asked me if I had a place, I told him yes, I had a place.

The Fine Art
of Sighing

〜〜〜〜〜〜〜〜〜〜〜

You feel a gradual welling up of pleasure, or boredom, or melancholy. Whatever the emotion, it's more abundant than you ever dreamed. You can no more contain it than your hands can cup a lake. And so you surrender and suck the air. Your esophagus opens, diaphragm expands. Poised at the crest of an exhalation, your body is about to be unburdened, second by second, cell by cell. A kettle hisses. A balloon deflates. Your shoulders fall like two ripe pears, muscles slack at last.

My mother stared out the kitchen window, ashes from her cigarette dribbling into the sink. She'd turned her back on the rest of the house, guarding her own solitude. I'd tiptoe across the linoleum and fix my lunch without making a sound. Sometimes I saw her back expand, then heard her let loose one plummeting note, a sigh so long and weary it might have been her last. Beyond our backyard, above telephone poles and apartment buildings, rose the brown horizon of the city; across it glided an occasional bird, or the blimp that advertised Goodyear tires. She might have been drifting into the distance, or lamenting her separation from it. She might have been wishing she were somewhere else, or wishing she could be happy where she was, a middle-aged housewife dreaming at her sink.

My father's sighs were more melodic. What began as a somber sigh could abruptly change pitch, turn gusty and loose, and suggest by its very transformation that what begins in sorrow might end in relief. He could prolong the rounded vowel of *oy*, or let it ricochet like an echo, as if he were shouting in a tunnel or a cave. Where my mother sighed from ineffable sadness, my father sighed at simple things: the coldness of a drink, the softness of a pillow, or an itch that my mother, following the frantic map of his words, finally found on his back and scratched.

A friend of mine once mentioned that I was given to long and ponderous sighs. Once I became aware of this habit, I heard my father's sighs in my own and knew for a moment his small satisfactions. At other times, I felt my mother's restlessness and wished I could leave my body with my breath, or be happy in the body my breath left behind.

It's a reflex and a legacy, this soulful species of breathing. Listen closely: My ancestors' lungs are pumping like bellows, men towing boats along the banks of the Volga, women lugging baskets of rye bread and pike. At the end of each day, they lift their weary arms in a toast; as thanks for the heat and sting of vodka, their aahs condense in the cold Russian air.

At any given moment, there must be thousands of people sighing. A man in Milwaukee heaves and shivers and blesses the head of his second wife, who's not too shy to lick his toes. A judge in Munich groans with pleasure after tasting again the silky bratwurst she ate as a child. Every day, meaningful sighs are expelled from schoolchildren, driving instructors, forensic experts, certified public accountants, and dental hygienists, just to name a few. The sighs of widows and widowers alone must account for a significant portion of the carbon dioxide released into the atmosphere. Every time a girdle is removed, a foot is submerged in a tub of warm water, or a restroom is reached on a desolate road . . . you'd think the sheer velocity of it would create mistrals, siroccos, hurricanes; arrows should be swarming over satellite maps, weathermen talking a mile a minute, ties flapping from their necks like flags.

Before I learned that Venetian prisoners were led across it to their execution, I imagined that the Bridge of Sighs was a feat of invisible engineering, a structure vaulting above the earth, the girders and trusses, the stay ropes and cables, the counterweights and safety rails, connecting one human breath to the next.

Against Gravity

~~~~~~~~~~~~~~~~~~~~~~~~

The logo for Weight-Lifter's — biceps flexed inside a circle — appears on the gymnasium's stationery, the laminated membership cards, and the T-shirts sold at the front desk. It was designed by Bobby, the lover of the man who founded Weight-Lifter's in the 1960s, Ted Rowan. Ted encouraged Bobby to decorate the gym with other examples of his artwork, including an entire wall covered with crayon sketches of Mr. Olympia contestants. Thighs shined like glazed hams. Pectorals bulged like overstuffed luggage. Bobby worshiped these muscular men, every oiled, overwrought inch of them.

Inflated by steroids and nutritional supplements, Bobby himself was a gargantuan man, big-shouldered, heavy-footed, making up in density what he lacked in height. Determined as a tank, he rolled through the gym on his daily rounds, dropping dumbbells back on their racks with an earsplitting crash. He smacked open doors and caused the stairs to creak when he took them, as if every gesture, every trajectory of digit or limb, was meant to announce his presence, to proclaim his weight in the world.

His studly impression might have been more successful if it weren't for one startling fact: Bobby possessed the voice of a schoolgirl. No amount of steroid injections could deepen or disguise it. How odd it was to hear him chirp his incessant reprimands: "Use a towel if you're gonna sweat." "Put the weights back after you use them." When he walked through the room, it was as though a breathy, irritable girl were operating levers and pulleys from within a gigantic man-puppet.

Bobby understood that a strain of absurdity ran through his every action. On one hand, he behaved as if he were fully in control of the amusing effect brought on by the schism between his voice and his physique, and he exploited it with lavish, campy performances. Polishing the equipment with a chamois would turn into a dance of veils. He'd stir his hips, wave the chamois in the air with a flourish. "You may watch me," he'd squeak to a gaggle of onlookers, "but you may not touch."

On the other hand, the burden of absurdity made him edgy and defensive. He could interpret even a fleeting glance as criticism and was notorious for snapping at innocent bystanders. The seasoned members of the gym took Bobby's tantrums in stride — they ignored him completely to finish their reps — but novices were often the embarrassed objects of his wrath. One day, a new member leaned toward a mirror to adjust his contact lens. Thinking the boy was trying to observe him surreptitiously, that his furrowed brows were a sign of condescension, Bobby spun on his heel, and hissed, "Checking your eyes for jaundice, honey? Hepatitis is rampant these days. Better be careful who fucks your butt."

It was not uncommon for men at the gym to discuss Bobby's outrageous behavior when he wasn't around; broaching the subject while he was on duty would be to risk his overhearing, and there was no telling what swift and unforgiving humiliation would follow. I'd been a member of the gym for several years and had always wondered how Ted, ten years Bobby's senior, the quieter, less muscular member of the duo, tolerated his lover's cantankerous public displays. Wasn't venom bad for business? Were steroids to blame? It was rumored that Ted had met Bobby while cruising Griffith Park in his Eldorado convertible. Their romantic history was, loosely speaking, a Pygmalion story:

Bobby was fresh from the Midwest, an undernourished hustler with a knack for art, an interest in bodybuilding, and an addiction to heroin. Ted skirted him off to his split-level house in the Hollywood Hills, fell head over heels (or "heels over head," as Bobby used to say), and got him into a detox program. Soon Bobby was made a full partner at the gym and settled into his current role as monolith and curiosity. It was clear from the way Ted chuckled at his boyfriend's outbursts that nothing would be done to stop them any time soon.

After his shifts at the front desk, Bobby would often retreat to the tanning room, jingling the two free tokens that gave him not the usual twenty-five minutes, but a fifty-minute dose of electric leisure. His perpetual tan was impressive, especially in winter. But it was also artificial and slightly orange, the tint of a chicken left too long under a heat lamp at the supermarket. Balding in his early thirties, he kept his hair short, the buzz cut lending his otherwise bland features a military severity. Judging from appearance alone, you would believe Bobby to be a man with an arid inner life, and perhaps that's what made his steady artistic output so surprising.

One day, in the glass case adjacent to the front desk, next to jars of Gainers Fuel and bottles of amino acids, there appeared Bobby's handmade, balsa wood models of a bench press, incline and decline bench, each with small barbells propped above them. They were painted in precise detail: silver enamel for metal, matte brown for the padded leather seats.

A month or two later, a freer, more inventive species of Bobby's art appeared next to the drinking fountain, across from the shower stalls, and above the front desk. These were acrylic paintings that included a wide array of "spiritual" imagery: pyramids, rainbows, unicorns, the vast blackness of outer space dotted with bright and habitable planets. It was as though Bobby had turned away from the immediate environment of the gym and was looking elsewhere, or inward, for a source of inspiration.

This aesthetic shift came at a time when Bobby was plagued by a succession of lingering colds. His high voice turned nasal, and his nose, despite the indelible tan, became chafed and red. He kept wadded Kleenex in the pocket of his sweatpants. Soon the flulike symptoms included headaches, soreness in his muscles, loss of appetite. Bobby's doctor advised him to cut out steroids until his body had time to recuperate. Without anabolics, Bobby lost the bulk that had once made him conspicuous. His mood grew steady. No longer was he prone to sideshows of improvisation or rage. He lost his talent for quips and insults. In fact, he went about his duties, dusting counters, updating memberships, with a remoteness that made him seem, for the first time in anyone's memory, preoccupied.

All of us who went to Weight-Lifter's suspected that Bobby had contracted AIDS, whether or not we registered it consciously or said it aloud. But this was in the early 1980s, when we were just beginning to toss and turn in the bad dream this disease would become, and we hoped against hope his colds were really colds. In a hotbed of gossip, Bobby grew worse. Pyramids and rainbows hung on the walls, *memento mori* for all their naive optimism. Even if we didn't like him (most of us didn't), the ways in which he had been insufferable seemed, at worst, misguided and benign, his illness unfair. When he finally stopped coming to the gym altogether, his absence was like the silence after a pistol report — ringing, deep, uneasy.

Ted began to disappear from Weight-Lifter's for long periods, tending the boy he'd found in the park. Once or twice he ran in to sign a check or to OK a delivery, but his eyes were ringed with sleeplessness, and he wore the dazed, bereft expression of a man who'd misplaced his fate.

Rumors began to circulate that Bobby had been admitted to the hospital, blind and raving from the pressure of a brain tumor. One day Lyle Barker, the bodybuilder who worked the desk during Bobby's absence, was asked to thank everyone on Ted's behalf for their concern and to assure us that Bobby's tumor was not a complication of AIDS. A short, stocky fireplug of a man, Lyle delivered the news with dutiful enthusiasm, often telling the same person twice. You could see visible relief on the faces of some men when they heard, as if, compared to viral havoc, tumors were a day at the beach. Others of us, however, were skeptical, wondering whether Ted insisted that Bobby didn't have AIDS because the possibility was unbearable, or because the news might frighten prospective members. Whatever the reason, our speculation didn't matter. Bobby was dead in a matter of days.

His voluminous bulk, his capacity to bench-press two fifty, the way his lumbering shook the walls, made us all the more incredulous that he was gone. Just yesterday, it seemed, he had taunted a formidable lifter who struggled to finish a bench press. As the man groaned and gasped for air, arms quivering from the strain of the weight, Bobby bent over, peered between the lifter's legs, and sang in a delicate doily of a voice, "I see Paris, I see France, I can see your underpants . . ."

*

In 1975, long before Weight-Lifter's, I belonged to Matt Morris' Gym. It was the first gym I'd ever joined, a place of fabled transformations. Scrawny men walked in through one door and swaggered out the other, pneumatic with muscle. Located in West Hollywood, its clientele was primarily gay. The gym was run by the namesake himself, an African American whose bodybuilding trophies, a whole periodic table of alloys, gleamed on the shelves behind his desk. A baroque piece of furniture as big as a barge, the desk looked cumbersome and incongruous amid all that sleek metal equipment. It sat, along with the owner, near the entrance to the gym, a high-ceilinged room with cinder block walls. Matt Morris oversaw all the goings-on in the echoing workout room. Although he never reacted overtly to the deafening clang of a dropped weight or the sudden eruption of camp among the members ("Pump it, girl!"), he glowed, for all his stoicism, with paternal light. The place was his baby.

Matt Morris spoke and moved slowly, deliberately, as if he were trying to conserve energy for some daunting task ahead. He handed me a contract that explained the terms of annual membership and exempted the gym from liability should I injure myself on the premises. I signed, but not without picturing myself pinned beneath a barbell, chest collapsing, face turning blue. "Let's take a look," he said, by which I thought he meant take a tour of the gym. Object of admiring glances, he walked across a room without so much as one frayed edge of self-consciousness. Muscles shifted beneath his shirt. He led me into the locker room. "Strip," he said, inspecting his fingernails. I wasn't sure I'd heard him correctly. "Take off your clothes," he enunciated, looking up at me long enough to give his request emphasis. "Let's see what we got so I know what kind of program to give you."

I don't think I would have obeyed so readily if it weren't for the fact that he'd said "see what *we* got." A dab of a word, a crumb of connection. I brightened at the idea that I was somehow a part of the bigness that was him.

Stripping, however, was easier in concept than in fact. Just determining the order in which my clothes would be peeled, and acting blasé while I peeled them, was no small feat. I was twenty-four years old at the time, but memories of the towel snappings, forgotten locker combinations, and catcalls from my junior high gym class came flooding back. By stripping I risked my mentor's disapproval; my soft stomach, my sloped shoulders — he would scrutinize the inadequacies my clothes had hidden. I bought time by folding my socks and setting my shoes down side by side. Matt Morris looked me up and down, aiming toward me the high beam of his professional assessment. He slipped from his back pocket a piece of paper that I imagined to be some kind of scorecard. I barely had my shirt unbuttoned before he jotted a couple of notes. How did I fare? What did I look like? I lost all sense of my body and momentarily turned into a vapor of pure curiosity. I strained to see what he had written, but panic hampered my vision. The air was humid from sweating men. Two beauties without towels passed me on their way to the shower, their cocks bobbing up and down, their immodesty exotic. Matt Morris cleared his throat. I returned, grudgingly, to my senses and undid my belt. My jeans turned inside out as I tried to step out of them. One leg caught my foot and tightened as I tried to free it, exasperating as the Chinese finger prison I played with as a child. I finally extracted a matching set of pale legs. Matt Morris paused and chewed his pencil. More notes were scrawled. I remember asking if I should take off my underpants. Perspiration trickled from my armpits. "Just turn around slowly, please." As I turned, a disco hit throbbed through the locker room, a barrage of orgasmic oohs and aahs. The idea of musical accompaniment while I spun in a circle, judged by a humorless giant with a scorecard, forced me to fight back nervous laughter.

"Legs," he said after I'd changed into shorts and a T-shirt. "Legs are your weakness." In the time it took me to change, he'd devised a plan for my metamorphosis. A typed card listed the exercises that, performed three days a week and combined with restrictions on fats and alcohol, were guaranteed to give me visible results in six weeks. His first vague smile came when I warned him that I didn't want to get *too* big. "I wouldn't worry

about that just yet. Proportion," he explained, "is more important than bulk, at least for a beginner. We're gonna blitz your legs
for starters. The rest of you can blow up later."

Hack squats were the first order of business. I had never done
them, and felt nothing but dread after I watched a demonstration. The man who showed them to me, a former Mr. Orange
County, had what appeared to be surgical bandages wrapped
around his knees. "Some knees can't take the strain," he informed me. "They crack like walnuts. Lots of guys wrap their
joints for protection." He backed into the squat rack and gripped
a barbell. With the bar balanced on the nape of his neck, he
lowered himself into a sitting position, ass cantilevered. His face
flushed and the veins in his neck bulged as he lifted himself
upright. The muscles in his thighs shifted and rippled, exposing
highlights and striations that had remained hidden when his legs
were at rest. In the last agonized seconds of effort, he looked
toward the sky. His expression of hideous, pop-eyed bliss made
me believe he'd seen the face of God.

Mr. Orange County let the barbell crash back onto the rack.
He took a moment to catch his breath and pick at the yellow
calluses that covered his palms. Then he and Matt Morris removed from either end of the barbell several forty-five-pound
plates. The denuded barbell didn't look nearly as intimidating as
it had a moment ago. "We'll start with nothing," said Matt Morris, which sounded apt and philosophical. I took my position at
the squat rack, braced my back against the length of the barbell, felt the chill of metal on the nape of my neck. Matt Morris
took my hands and placed them in the appropriate grip. He
smelled of an after-shave that I guessed was emerald green. He
straightened my posture and widened my stance with the warm,
insistent pressure of his paws. I concentrated on the moist work-
ings of his tongue and lips as well as on his sage advice. If this
had been a fantasy, I'd have found myself aroused. But I was too

self-conscious to enjoy his scent and attention. The room grew busy with the afternoon crowd, and I tried to bolster my courage by repeating to myself, *No one is watching me, no one cares*, precisely the lack of attention that drove me to a gym in the first place.

I managed to lurch forward with the barbell propped on my shoulders, as proud as a toddler of my first step. Matt Morris hovered behind me. When he urged me "Down," I let my knees flex and slowly lowered my pelvis, fire spreading inside my thighs. "Keep breathing," he ordered. I wasn't aware that I'd ceased to breathe, and now had to concentrate on inflating my lungs as well as on bending my legs, which felt rubbery and new. I sucked the air. My knees quivered. Bright spots swam in the corners of my eyes.

I had always taken for granted that my body was stacked a certain way: calves rise from ankles, torso rides waist, head rests upon neck. Then, poof, my parts were out of whack, the arrangement of my flesh and bones a mere theory to be disproved. Tendons bent. Muscles buckled. Joints hinged inward. My buttocks plummeted earthward and landed on my ankles. My knees, pinpoints of pain, pressed against my chest. I fell so fast, even Matt Morris didn't have the reflexes to catch me. I hunkered in a crouch from which I couldn't unfold. Locked into place on the floor of the gym, I still held the barbell behind my back, arms clamped to my sides. Mr. Orange County relieved me of the barbell. Matt Morris lifted me up by my armpits, restoring me to the posture of Homo sapiens.

People whispered. People pointed. People looked. My virgin hack squat left me both literally and metaphorically crushed. Matt Morris seemed thrown by my sudden crumpling and coddled me from that point on. "The bar alone weighs almost thirty pounds," he said to spare me. It was too late. What happened afterward I remember only as whispered instruction, muffled music, pain in different body parts, and an abstract swirl of other men. In the midst of every exercise, I craved a cigarette.

The session ended with Matt Morris filing my program in an alphabetized card catalogue. He apologized for not catching my fall and suggested a hot sitz bath to reduce any tenderness in my knees and glutes. "I wanna see you here at least three times a week," he called after me. "No pain, no gain."

I couldn't bring myself to shower in the locker room, not until weightlifting chiseled my limbs and put a stop to my modesty. I may not even have continued at the gym, so perfect and discouraging did the bodies of other members seem, if I hadn't met Terry Cahalan on my way out. I was zipping my gym bag when a man opened the locker next to mine. In the periphery of my vision, I was struck by an impression of extreme paleness. His translucent skin, fine hair, and hazel eyes were leached of color. Terry was not, technically speaking, albino, but he bore the washed-out countenance of an overexposed photograph. Like all the men I'd seen that day, Terry was huge. Pale blue veins webbed his forearms and hairless thighs; his skin made him appear delicate and vulnerable, despite his scale. His cheeks were pink from the heat of the shower. His scalp gleamed like an eggshell through tendrils of matted hair. I half expected to see his heart, a shadow pulsing behind his breastbone.

It was he who initiated conversation. Terry had gone to film school, and told me that Ingmar Bergman was the director he most admired. Our disagreement about Bergman (I mocked his soundtracks of ticking clocks) turned into playful sparring. There seemed to be no pause, no mediation, between Terry's thoughts and their articulation. He reddened when he laughed, watched me closely as I talked, nodded whenever he agreed with what I'd said. Even after Terry dressed he seemed naked, readable, his interest in me overt.

Physically, I was everything he was not: thin, hirsute, darkercomplected, a Russian Jew to his Irish Catholic. Our polarity promised sexual adventure; we could wrestle away our differences. We made plans to meet for dinner that night.

Over vegeburgers, Terry introduced me to the vocabulary of bodybuilding. We discussed supersetting versus fewer reps at a heavier weight, free weights versus Universal machines, carboloading versus protein powder, definition versus density. The attention he paid to the minutiae and nuance of the male form was like slow, taunting foreplay. Asking to pass the salt became charged with innuendo. By the time we walked through the door to my apartment, I vibrated with excitement, as if I'd spent hours on a train and could still feel the phantom jolts of motion. A sense of urgency preceded all my sexual encounters in those days, a mixture of intense longing and the apprehension that I might disappoint. Undressing in front of Terry promised to be as challenging as undressing in front of Matt Morris. In fact, that night Terry wore a Matt Morris T-shirt. He sprawled on the living room couch, my trainer's name stretched across his chest, the fabric rippling with suggestive shadows.

A reading lamp bathed one side of Terry's face. I dove for the dark side, licking the salty length of his throat. He lay back and let me kiss him. Only after my initial excitement subsided did I realize Terry hadn't budged. I drew back to catch my breath and saw that he wore an unwavering, grateful expression. During the next descent I became aware of my lapping sounds, amplified in the silence of the night. The clock ticked audibly, as in an Ingmar Bergman movie. With my face still nuzzling his neck, I put my hand against his chest. He held it there with passionate force, but in such a way that massaging or exploring him further would have been impossible without pushing his hand away. I drew back once again. His expression remained unchanged, a marble bust of utter contentment. His eyes were shut, the fringe of his lashes gold in the lamplight. "Terry," I whispered.

"Yes," he said, eyes shut tight.

"Do you want to, you know, go into the bedroom?"

"Yes," he said. His voice was dreamy and thin, an assent from a distant world.

I took his hand and pulled him to his feet. He opened his eyes and strode into the bedroom without the slightest hesitation. His eagerness surprised me; I'd begun to worry that he was having second thoughts. He fixed me in a steady gaze, stepped out of his jeans and underpants, and kicked them away. They skidded across the wooden floor. He drew the T-shirt over his head, struggling photogenically. His armpits and groin were an impossible shade whiter than the rest of his body. He stood naked and waiting, a moonlit apparition.

I fought the urge to implode as I undressed; surely Terry was accustomed to the stunning specimens at the gym. I forced myself to act uninhibited; pretence, I guessed, was better than self-consciousness. Once I was naked, I turned around to toss my clothes onto a nearby chair. When I turned back, Terry had lifted both arms above his head in a languorous yawn. The tension of the stretch elongated his torso and showed, to moonlit advantage, the development of his biceps. Once he was sure I had noticed or, more accurately, once he was sure I had noticed and registered admiration, he began to nuzzle his upper arm, brushing the apex of the muscle with his lips as if trying not to kiss it took all his self-restraint. His eyes slowly closed, that gentle, beatific grin playing over his face. I thought this fondling might be a method, like rubbing one's cock, that he used to arouse himself. But Terry stayed flaccid. This show of inscrutable sensuality continued for several seconds, so private at times, I wasn't sure my being there was necessary.

On one hand, I found Terry's posing erotic. I'd never seen anyone touch themselves with such ardor. I could hear, in the courtyard of my Spanish apartment, the splashing of a fountain that recirculated a single spray of water, the effect hypnotic and lovely, not unlike my date's performance. On the other hand, I wanted Terry to vanquish my sense of physical inadequacy with a show of enthusiasm, and it was already clear that we were destined to spend the night vying for each other's attention.

"Terry," I whispered. He opened his eyes. "Let's get into bed." He dove onto the sheets, threw his arms above his head, closed his eyes, and simply resumed the previous pose while laying on his back. My bed at the time was a foam pad on top of a piece of plywood, the legs four logs I'd bought as firewood. I sat by Terry's side. Our combined weight strained the plywood. Every time I shifted position, licking Terry's nipples or running my hands along his side, the bed creaked and groaned like a ship in rough seas. Though the sex we were having was cautious and tame, it must have sounded like a bacchanalia to my downstairs neighbor. Touching Terry required a degree of deliberation and tact that all but doused the fire of excitement. He bit his wrist, rubbed his stomach, concentrating on his anatomy as intently as someone working a crossword puzzle; I didn't want to interrupt him. Still, he was pretty to look at, and there came a modicum of encouragement whenever his big, sleepy penis rose for a second, then lolled to one side. Please look at me, I wanted to say whenever he grew hard, so I might believe he was stirred by the sight of me.

He burrowed the back of his head into the pillow and caressed the lobes of his shoulders. His sensuous introversion was, I began to suspect, the result of an embarrassment greater than mine. As long as Terry clung to the rewards of his own beauty, he was safe from the consequences of human contact, sustained by sensations that he alone controlled.

We manipulated ourselves to orgasm, each in a separate reverie. I came first, then petted him and waited. He stroked himself with brutal rapidity. The instant before he ejaculated, his eyes sprang open. He stared at the ceiling, lost in astonishment. It was as if he could see through plaster and beams to the stars suspended above the city. I could feel the wake of him leaving his body, his chest and stomach flushing with blood. I braced for his cry of release or satisfaction — to drift from the self for one blessed second — but he came without sound, his contraction brief and taut as a sob.

In the lull that followed, Terry held me, our contentment like sketchy parallel lines. If sex with Terry hadn't been as fulfilling and acrobatic as I'd hoped, at least there was the consolation of a man's flesh pressed next to mine. We listened to the fountain splash. Suddenly, Terry laughed without provocation, causing the bed to creak. "It would never," he said, "work out between us." I bristled, believing that if our sex had been misguided, comical, or bland, the fault was not mine. At least I'd done him the honor of keeping my eyes open. "Oh, now, don't get all bent out of shape," he said, sensing I'd taken offense. He tightened his embrace. "I meant it as a compliment. None of my relationships have ever lasted anyway. This way we get to be friends."

At that point, I wasn't so sure Terry and I were meant to be friends. But we continued to run into each other at the gym, to talk about movies and books. Eventually, Terry gave me one of his scripts to read. I gave him a sheaf of my poems. We began to critique each other's work on a regular basis. Went to the Laundromat together. The library. Shared preparations for Saturday nights.

Before we went to dinner, or to a bar, or manhunting at a discotheque, Terry would model for me his spectrum of skintight shirts. Tank tops, T-shirts, Izods. Often it seemed that he rummaged through his entire wardrobe, swatches of fabric arcing through the air. Shedding his clothes at every opportunity remained one of Terry's nervous habits, like cracking one's knuckles or snapping gum. As Terry writhed free from a clinging shirt, I played the role of captive audience as well as fashion consultant. Adding to the theatrical ambience was the fact that Terry lived like a spartan; his bedroom's only furnishings were a mattress on the floor and a gooseneck lamp that he twisted this way and that in order to shine the most flattering light on his sartorial marathons.

Terry knew as many methods for improving one's appearance as Heloise knew household hints. He sewed the armholes to one shirt an inch smaller, the elastic tight as a tourniquet, making his biceps bulge even more. When he felt that he had overeaten at dinner, we'd drive back to his apartment before preceding to a bar so he could change from a tapered V-neck into a Beefy-T. Once I caught him in the dank bathroom of a leather bar, peering into a clouded mirror and lightly rubbing his nipples so the tips would show through his shirt.

Terry Cahalan fervently believed in the enticements of the flesh. I paid attention, his rapt apprentice, hoping some of his self-regard would rub off on me. Of all the diminishments of living in the closet, one of the most insidious is the way it robs a man of his body; lust is denied again and again until the instrument of lust is itself denied. The fuss of those days, it seems to me in retrospect, was a way of reinventing our bodies, limb by limb, like restless gods.

It had gotten to the point where I couldn't go shopping without my friend in tow; when choosing pants and shoes and glasses, I depended on the lightning strike of his definitive opinion. While advising me on some new purchase, Terry would often interrupt himself in midsentence to announce that my arms had grown thicker or my lats a little wider than the last time he'd looked. One night he suggested taking my measurements for posterity; this way I'd have a record of my progress. His request seemed as sentimental as asking for a lock of my hair and testified to his faith that I'd one day outgrow my skinny stature. He retrieved a cloth tape measure from his sewing kit and we went into his bedroom. He twisted the lamp till it shined an egg of light against the wall. I stripped to my underwear, happy to feel my modesty fading. Terry lowered himself to his knees, encircled my leg with the tape measure, and pinched it closed around my calf. I peered down at his massive shoulders, his colorless hair. What were we, I wondered, to one another? Our familiarity with each other's bodies, the dailiness of our routines, the giving of advice that was at once brotherly and sisterly — on the sliding scale from strangers to spouses our relationship resisted definition. Terry recorded my measurements on a piece of notebook paper. For the sake of accuracy, he was careful to find the anatomical center of every muscle group from calves to neck. He grazed my limbs with his hands, his hair, the pressure of his breath. The summer night was so temperate and still that it was hard to tell where my skin left off and the world began.

Not only did Terry notice and remark on each small sign of my improvement, he suggested ways to make my exercises more effective. "Remember not to lock your elbows." "Go slow on the negative." "Drink lots of water." He badgered me about the days I missed my workout or simply slacked off. He oversaw every phase of my indoctrination into physical culture except for one: he'd never actually train with me. Our camaraderie ended at the threshold of the gym. Terry couldn't abide the idea of social interaction, however amiable or slight, interfering with his concentration on the weights.

When we happened to visit Matt Morris' at the same time, Terry's eyes flicked past me. He neither waved nor said hello. His oblivion was democratic; he reacted to everyone with the blank expression of an amnesiac. Overcoming gravity and maintaining good form was all that mattered. Terry loaded the bars with weights. He grunted and strained. After each exertion, he scowled into the middle distance, shaking out a cramp in his leg or toweling sweat from the back of his neck. On rare occasions, as he finished a lift, he let out the tentative curse of a lapsed Catholic. By now I had grown confident enough to use the shower and the steam room; sometimes I'd glimpse him through a scalding cloud, perched on a tier of white tile, pensive as Rodin's *Thinker.* I knew enough to leave Terry alone at those moments, certain that later the same evening, at dinner or a bar, he would be his garrulous, forthcoming self. I'd grown accustomed to, even fascinated by, Terry's periods of insularity. Alternations of warmth and aloofness were the rhythm by which he moved through the world.

Terry searched aggressively for a boyfriend, yet opted for a series of one-night stands. These were men whom I rarely met but heard about later. It was not uncommon during our visits to a bar for Terry to point to someone through the haze of cigarette smoke and then shout into my ear, over the roar of music and laughter, the details of their encounter. I'd hold the unsuspecting man in my gaze while my eardrum buzzed with the bass notes of gossip. If the date hadn't progressed to sex, Terry would tell me why. Perhaps the man was a misogynist, or thought it might be fun to shave Terry's pubic hair, or mentioned he was a Republican. There were any number of quirks or proclivities that might disqualify a prospective partner. Terry's rigorous discrimination, however, also applied to those men with whom he did have sex. One had been loving but needed to work on his body. "Call me shallow," Terry said in his own defense, "but when a guy's body is too smooth and soft, I don't feel like I'm making it with a man." Another might have been sufficiently "hairy and barbaric," but lacked ambition and showed no interest in art.

In all our conversations, I never once had the heart to ask Terry about the most likely reason that relationships eluded him: his narcissism. I was afraid he'd be hurt by the implication that I'd found sex with him eerie or inadequate, and that others might too. Every time I considered raising the possibility that the intimacy he sought was incompatible with posing, I stopped myself, figuring there was no good reason why Terry couldn't find a devoted lover whose deepest needs were satisfied by the sight of a Catholic boy flexing in the buff. Besides, I needed to commiserate with someone about the difficulty of finding a boyfriend; I often found the search exhausting and futile myself, like trying to jog across town on a treadmill. Paralyzed in high school by the knowledge that we were queer, neither Terry nor I had had much experience dating. The nights we now spent at discotheques and bars had about them a sense of wild improvisation, as if the rituals of romance that had been denied us were being invented belatedly. We made up for lost time and wrote the rules to fit our whims. Without precedent or model, our affairs were like tree houses — fantastic, precarious, jerry-built.

I met a truck driver with one tan arm; his vigorous kisses tasted like coffee; he held me with the grip of a man who watches cities slip past a windshield. I met an accountant who wore his reading glasses to bed; during nights of slow, methodical sex, the luminous numbers of a digital clock were reflected in his lenses. After purchasing seed packets at a Pasadena nursery, I was led by the owner to a house behind an arbor; his bedroom smelled of turned earth; his body felt as hard as mahogany.

With each man I met there came a moment — as he undid his shirt, as his breathing quickened, as a look of expectancy claimed his face — when he endeared himself by being alive beside me. I'm embarrassed to admit it now, but there also came moments of great disappointment when I never saw the man again, or saw him again and realized that we had nothing but sexual attraction in common. I remember Terry telling me, not unkindly, that I was naive to think of every man I met as a prospective lover. He compared me to a newborn duckling who trusts and follows the first thing he sees. "You need," he advised, "to develop thicker skin." "That's ironic," I teased him, "coming from you," meaning from someone huge and translucent.

During the first year of knowing Terry, our sexual adventures made fodder for conversation, but they never posed a threat to our friendship. Until I met Bill Bader.

Bill's ambition was to become an "avowedly homosexual" comedian. During the days, he worked at a series of temporary jobs, from pool cleaner to file clerk. At night, in the living room of his small apartment in Hollywood, he stood on the hearth of the fireplace, a makeshift stage, and perfected the routine with which he would one day make his debut. Whenever I came to visit, I could hear him practicing as I walked up the flagstone path that led to his front door and could see him through the living room window, dressed in sweats, his curly hair unkempt. Before I knocked on the door, I'd stop and watch him go through his paces. He cleared his throat, tested inflections. "In *Greece*, how do they separate the men from the boys?" A moment of silent consideration. "How *do* they separate the men from the boys in Greece?" Bill repeated the same gag over and over, delivering the punch line — "with a crowbar" — in tones ranging from an absolute deadpan to the zeal of someone winning at bingo.

Though he'd never touched a cigarette, Bill had the ragged voice of a chain-smoker, and the wryest delivery of anyone I had ever known. He spoke mostly out of the right side of his mouth. His every comment — "nice shirt," "the coffee is cold" — seemed laden with ironic force. When I told Bill that he had the power to make anything sound absurd, he retrieved the yellow pages and began to reel off names (Shawn Lamont, Audrey Lapine) with a disbelief that suggested these couldn't possibly be the names of human beings, unless their parents had been drunk or insane.

Bill asked me to coach him on the appropriate gestures and facial expressions to go with each joke: shrugs, sighs, the arching of his eyebrows, the rolling of his eyes. I'm not sure I was much help, growing overanalytical as quickly as he did. The rigors of comedy, polishing each line while retaining its freshness, resembled the rigors of writing, and I considered Bill an artist. He wrestled with an imaginary microphone stand, practiced raising his hand to quell applause. Watching Bill rehearse was a constant reminder of what it was that drew me to him: like me, Bill was a recent convert to exercise; he moved with a surprised delight, as if he had just been given his body and was learning what it could say and do.

I'd met Bill on the roof deck of the Holiday Health Spa, a scattering of chaise longues on a vast expanse of AstroTurf. Even from the seventh floor of the high-rise that housed the gym, you could hear the shouts of tourists who arrived by the busload on Hollywood Boulevard below. Bill flopped onto a chaise next to mine. Without so much as introducing himself, he began a running commentary on the sunbathers. A blond man lying next to us, tan and slathered with oil, had taken two slices of cucumber from a Tupperware container and placed them over his eyes. "Add vinegar," Bill muttered, "and toss him lightly." Woozy from the heat, I felt particularly susceptible to Bill's jokes. My laughter egged him on. "Look," he exclaimed when another man arrived in skintight shorts, "I can read the date on the dime in his pocket." The sun burned through a pall of smog. Bill turned on his back, closed his eyes, and continued talking. I stared at his chest and stomach and thighs.

I'd left Matt Morris' because the standards of physical perfection that inspired Terry Cahalan had begun to depress me. I'd walk into the gym feeling relatively content about myself, but once inside, I'd lose perspective. The bigger lifters flaunted their physiques like ostentatious upholstered suits. When I glimpsed my reflection next to theirs, I felt like a wet Chihuahua. Vanity of this order required more effort and sacrifice than I was willing to make. One man, preparing for an amateur bodybuilding contest, would not allow himself a drink of water while he exercised for fear that he would become bloated and lose the "cuts" that gave his body the faceted geometry of a cubist painting. At the end of a punishing workout, his lips were as parched as someone who'd been wandering through the desert. Another member with the bald head and handlebar mustache of a circus strongman would gorge himself on a bucket of Kentucky Fried Chicken before every workout in order to bulk up. He left a film of sweat on the equipment, his chin glistening with grease. So many men trimmed the hair on their chests and backs and shoulders that it became impossible to distinguish those men who possessed naturally symmetrical patterns of body hair from the practitioners of an intimate topiary. In the late afternoon, the workout room would begin to reek of what I thought was the odor of raw hamburger wafting in from the coffee shop next door. Terry later told me it was the smell of men who injected steroids and sweated a hormonal musk, bitter and bovine. This explained, according to Terry, the outbreaks of acne among the members, the sudden astonishing gains in scale, and the air of imperiousness and aggression that colored the gym on certain days like a harsh cast of light.

By contrast, the Holiday Spa, with its coed membership and the varied ages and races of its clientele, was more like . . . a holiday. The casual tenor of the place made it easier for me to keep from berating myself and to distinguish, when it came to people's appearance, truth from illusion.

I ran into Bill at the gym almost every weekend. Late one afternoon we ended up side by side at a crowded bank of blow dryers. Bill told me he wanted to form a precision drill team of homosexuals who would march in formation while blow-drying their hair, the finale being a blizzard of sparks and a citywide blackout. Intrigued when he took a small notepad out of his gym bag to record what he'd said, I finally asked him out for coffee. When the waitress asked Bill what he wanted, he pointed at me, and said, "Him, on toast." From that day on, we saw each other often.

Bill was a package deal, so to speak; along with him I inherited the constant company of his previous boyfriend, Ron Marco, who had recently moved to California from New Jersey. Judging from Ron's appreciative laughter and constant show of concern, he was still a little smitten with Bill. The first night we met, Ron cornered me when Bill was out of the room. He shook my hand and told me to take good care of his buddy, who, for all his goofing around, was more sensitive than he appeared. Ron's gesture had about it an unmistakable formality, as if he were handing over to me, in some official capacity, the responsibilities of office. Auspicious as this moment had been, I didn't think of it again until months later when Bill bolted up in bed at three o'clock in the morning, teeth chattering, and swore he was losing his mind.

But for now, the three of us made a happy, if iconoclastic, family. On Friday nights, Bill and I waited at Ron's apartment — Bill still kept a key — for Ron to return from his job as a telephone lineman for Pacific Bell. At five-thirty, Ron would shoulder open the front door and clomp into the foyer in a pair of workboots. A cigarette dangled from his mouth, bobbing up and down and dribbling ash as he complained about his day. The subject of his complaints never varied; Ron's straight partner felt threatened by being assigned to a shift with a known homosexual and had said or done yet one more thing to illustrate his ignorance and disapproval. He tended not to talk to Ron, to cower against the door of the truck, and to misinterpret a friendly glance as an act of seduction. Railing against the man in a New Jersey accent ("Why would I wanna touch da guy? He's ugly as shit"), Ron would swagger into the living room, preceded by his barrel chest, and mix himself an orange blossom. Like a magic elixir, the pastel drink would gradually soften the rough edges of his mood. By the second round his posture had relaxed and he was ready to put up his feet and let go of his grudge until tomorrow. He'd remove the pack of Marlboros rolled in the sleeve of his T-shirt and unhook his pendulous tool belt, which fell to the carpet with a thud. Ron sank into a floral armchair and stared at us with gauzy fondness. "You boys must be hungry," he'd sigh, smoke wafting from his nostrils. No sooner had he gotten comfortable than he'd struggle to his feet, knees cracking, and disappear through a swinging door. In the kitchen, he'd don an apron and start mincing garlic for spaghetti sauce, a family recipe entrusted to him by his late mother.

Ron refused to let us help make dinner. While Bill and I listened to Vivaldi and hugged on the couch, he'd set his fine china and stemware on the table. Teary from onion fumes, he'd cast us a moist, approving glance. There was no hint of jealousy on Ron's part regarding my affection for his former boyfriend. He seemed to derive pleasure from the fact that Bill and I found his place a haven. Ron was a man who thought the world essentially rotten and unfair — an outlook his job confirmed — and he was determined to make his home a refuge from chaos, for his friends as well as for himself. He served us crackers on a lacquered tray, lit candles on the mantel, and told us to take a look at his newest books, *Renaissance Architecture Rediscovered* and *Masterpieces of the Japanese Kimono.*

Most people, judging Ron by his work clothes and his New Jersey accent, would have been surprised by his refinements. Despite his impressive physique, square jaw, hairy forearms, and swarthy skin, the feature he most wanted to be admired for were his luxurious eyelashes. He was active in his union, could repair broken radios and televisions, and drove an old Mustang convertible he restored himself, but his greatest wish was, in his words, "ta settle down and be the housewife I was born ta be."

Since Ron was the only man I knew who owned a feather duster and cleaned the grout in his bathroom with a toothbrush, his wish sounded plausible. As far as Bill and I were concerned, the paradoxes in Ron's interests and behavior enriched his character. I remember once telling Ron that he was androgynous ("Is it contagious?" Bill had asked), but in retrospect I see that I was wrong. Ron's male and female aspects coexisted, but remained as distinct as an apron and a tool belt.

Because he bore the weathered, menacing presence of a pirate or an army sergeant, Ron attracted men who wanted to be spanked, or to call him Daddy, or generally to have him take control, whereas Ron himself was looking for a husband to pamper and look up to, someone who could free him from his servitude to the telephone company and offer him a quiet home life. In public, he was instantly typecast as a brute or a stud and found it tiresome when men approached him with an expectation of stony, authoritarian masculinity. "Hey, handsome," one man said, sidling up to him at a bar and appraising his torso, "where'd you get those muscles?"

"Oh, these?" cooed Ron, hugging himself. "At Frederick's of Hollywood. Where'd you get yours?"

Bill wrote it down.

Terry Cahalan, who occasionally joined the three of us when we went barhopping, was impressed by Bill's dedication to his notebook. Terry respected the impulse to hoard the raw material of experience and turn it into art, and he assumed that people felt the same respect for him. Sitting next to Bill in the back seat of Ron's convertible, Terry regaled us with long, gloomy scenarios of the scripts he wanted to write. Weeping people and autumn leaves figured prominently in Terry's imagination. The plots tended toward betrayal, disillusionment, and loss in ostensibly happy families. While Terry described a dramatic camera pan or a character's chilling revelation, Ron shifted gears and tapped his fingers on the steering wheel in time to Top 40 songs. Bill leaned back and let the wind rush through his hair, staring up at the arc lights that lined the boulevards, a sulfurous yellow against the night. "Uh-huh, uh-huh," I would say periodically, so that Terry felt we were listening.

In the panoramic openness of Ron's convertible, a dozen sights begged for attention. The city jittered with insomniacs. Couples kissed or argued at bus stops. People waited in line to get inside a club before last call or congregated at the newsstands that dotted West Hollywood. Shirtless hustlers, high on amphetamines, paced the corners and craned their necks at passing traffic; they twitched and scratched and shifted their weight, as skittish as birds.

One night the four of us stopped at the Yukon Mining Company, an all-night coffee shop. With its Formica tables, vinyl seats, and fluorescent atmosphere, there was nothing remotely rustic about the place, unless you counted the photo blowup of a ghost town that hung above the cash register. Drunks slumped at the counter. Twin girls, no matter how many times their parents told them not to, dipped their French fries in a glass of ice water to cool them off. Two men wearing leather harnesses and studded armbands sucked the dregs of milk shakes through straws. A klatch of transvestites, resplendent in their beaded gowns and platinum wigs, sat at a table near the front door and evaluated in stage whispers the men who entered. Ron's compact build and five o'clock shadow inspired a collective intake of breath the moment we stepped through the door. Knowing the effect it would have, Bill turned and told them that Ron was a telephone lineman. Lashes fluttered, bracelets rattled, feathers floated from boas. There followed a slew of double entendres about climbing poles and the proper use of tools. Ron blushed and jammed his hands in his pocket, which caused them to swoon all the more.

The four of us squeezed into a bright orange booth. As we

waited for our order of pie and coffee, Terry continued telling us about his latest idea for a movie, picking up the plot where he had left off in the car: "And the camera pulls back farther and farther, and the street is deserted, and no lights are on in the Randalls' home except for the light in Jessica's room, and the night is dark, and the trees are bare, and the shot is like . . . a silent scream."

"*Garçon*," shouted Bill, snapping his fingers at the harried waiter, "bring this man an Academy Award before he drives us crazy."

Terry turned red and brooded. Unaware how hurtful his remark had been, Bill began to christen the male customers with drag names — Lily Pond, Velveeta Fondue, Crystal Knickknack — making Ron laugh so hard he started to hack uncontrollably.

And so began the rift between my friend and my lover. Terry's melancholy and Bill's sarcasm simply would not mix. During a screening of *The Candle*, Terry's thesis project for graduate school, Bill fidgeted, jiggled his foot, and sighed like a bored child. In the film, moths battered against a windowpane, killing or injuring themselves in their frenzy to find the source of light. This was intercut with images of a candle burning lower and lower. Judging from the arches in the background and the echo of a dirge, perhaps it was a votive candle in the shadowy recesses of some monastery. A towheaded boy wept into his pillow, but it was unclear whether he was in the monastery or in a suburban bedroom, an ambiguity that I wanted to believe was intentional. When a Catholic bishop, dressed in a miter and white vestments, floated toward the camera in slow motion and swung a smoking censer back and forth, Bill could stand it no longer. "Love your dress," he muttered to the screen, "but your purse is on fire." I elbowed him in the ribs, worried that Terry might hear. The towheaded boy curled into a fetal position. Drips of wax slid down the candle. A woman (the boy's mother?) stared pensively out a window (the window against which the moths were beating?), and one could see, reflected in the glass over her shoulder, the guttering candle finally go out. "*Fin*" appeared in the center of the screen.

When the lights went up, the small audience blinked and rustled and broke into appreciative applause. Martina, a willowy actress with whom Terry had gone to school, walked to the front of the screening room and introduced him, saying he would be happy to answer any questions from the audience, which consisted primarily of former professors and classmates. The questions tended toward the technical — "What f-stop did you use for the candlelight?" "How did you keep from getting the reflection of your camera in the windowpane?" — though Terry found a way to interject aesthetics. He told us, for example, that he'd used a recording of startled pigeons taking flight for the fluttering of the moths because "the sound embodied both panic and escape." This made a kind of lyrical sense to me, but I couldn't look at Bill for fear of finding him with his mouth twisted to one side, ready to let loose a sardonic comment.

Terry, on the other hand, acted as if he were at a funeral the night of Bill's debut at the Comedy Shop. He and Ron and I got there early and sat at a small, wobbly table near the stage. We ordered tart green margaritas and listened to pop tunes booming over the loudspeakers. Ron chain-smoked, played with the cocktail napkin, and glanced at his watch. Terry and I looked around as people filed into the room and rushed to find decent seats. Then they folded their arms or squeezed their dates, staring toward the empty stage. It was amateur night. Bill, who had been "psyching up" backstage, dashed out to tell us that he had gotten the seventh spot when numbers had been drawn from a hat earlier that evening. "Maybe not missionary," he said, "but a really good position." He vanished when the lights dimmed, and the master of ceremonies, a fat man with frizzy hair and a Hawaiian shirt, waddled up to the microphone. His odd walk produced a smattering of chuckles, a fact he either enjoyed or resented, it was hard to tell which. He grabbed the microphone off its stand — feedback shrieked — and announced, without a trace of enthusiasm, the names of the comedians who were scheduled to appear in the month to come. Then he made his way to the edge of the stage and proceeded to warm up the crowd. "What's your name, honey," he asked a pretty blond woman drinking a beer. She froze in midsip, a deer caught in headlights. "Candy," she said, almost inaudibly. "And what flavor are you, Candy?" An isolated laugh from the back of the room. The emcee winked at Candy, stuck out his tongue, and licked the air. Her date stiffened like a model in a Sears catalogue.

Ron tore open another pack of Marlboros. I laughed as the emcee lobbed insults into the audience, but my laughter was a kind of camouflage meant to help me blend in and prevent me from becoming his next target. "There's so much pain in that man's face," Terry said of the emcee, an observation he would repeat each time the man walked onto the stage, squinted at an index card, and introduced a new comic.

Most of the performers mocked their body parts or the body parts of their spouses. "I keep my toupee in a cage lined with newspaper," one man began. Another opened with, "My wife, Annie Oakley, has saddlebags." The laughter was grudging. As the evening progressed and booze was consumed, the audience grew boisterous, demanding, and quick to judge, a rumbling volcano that could only be appeased by the sacrifice of fresh performers. Bad puns met with collective groans. Cries of "You stink" and "Keep your day job" were frequent and vehement. Barbs from the audience elicited more laughter than most of the jokes. "This is a Roman circus," whispered Terry. From our vantage point at the front of the room, we could see hands tremble, foreheads perspire, and careers snuffed out before they had begun. The performers usually ended their acts by shouting, with

varying degrees of insincerity, "You've been a great audience!"
Each time a comic walked off stage, the flimsy curtain rippled
behind him, an ethereal farewell.

The emcee introduced the sixth performer. She wore a gigantic muumuu. Her voice sounded like two balloons being
rubbed together. Having mastered an expression of absolute baf-
flement, her shtick depended on convincing the audience that
the simplest tasks — frying an egg, answering the phone — were
as complex to her as higher mathematics. She might as well have
been speaking Latin; during her routine I buzzed with apprehension; Bill was up next.

My pulse was pounding so hard when the emcee introduced
him that it felt as if my hands and feet had hearts. Ron shot me a
look that said, Was this a mistake? What can we do? Too late, it
occurred to me that Bill would have been safer testing his material at a gay bar or nightclub. I had become so focused on the
details of his act — what should he wear? should he cut the last
joke? — that the potential for a homophobic reaction hadn't occurred to me. Relentless practice had made Bill confident, so I
had felt confident, too. Until I sat in the audience. I scanned the
dark room to see if there were any tables of gay men or lesbians
who might be receptive to Bill's material, and saw an indistinct
sea of hostility.

And then he stood center stage, his delivery as wry as ever. He
told the one about the drill team of queers with blow dryers. He
told the one about the gay guy whose pants were so tight you
could read the date on the dime in his pocket. He told joke after
joke in smooth succession. The audience, I realized, wasn't sure
at first whether Bill was making fun of homosexuals or was a
homosexual himself. This ambiguity seemed to intrigue the
crowd and forced them to pay attention. The laughter was
steady, if reticent. Things changed, however, once Bill told jokes
that made clear his sexual orientation. "I was talking to this old

boyfriend of mine . . ." and "Have you ever kissed a man with a mustache?" The atmosphere grew edgy and uncertain. The more liberal members of the audience may have felt guilty about laughing at a homosexual. And those who would ordinarily be happy to ridicule homosexuals resented Bill for usurping their power to instigate that ridicule.

Terry hugged himself. Ron spewed more smoke into the air than a brushfire. I found myself forcing a laugh, each "ha" a boulder I had to roll uphill.

Bill persevered, blinded by the spotlight, his material falling flat. He must have seen only darkness before him, a darkness in which he heard throats being cleared, coins change hands, and ice cubes chime, each moment of silence as vast as outer space. The instant he finished, the three of us clapped, a salvo of applause meant to compensate for the less-than-enthusiastic response from the rest of the audience, who clapped listlessly and shifted in their seats. Bill heard the ruckus and squinted in our general direction. When he handed the microphone back to the emcee, he pinched the man's cheek, a spontaneous touch for which we later congratulated him.

"They should call that place the Tragedy Shop," Terry said on the drive home. Laughter's underpinning of pain was just the kind of paradox Terry found delicious.

"Once I got up there," Bill insisted, "it wasn't that bad." He leaned back in the seat. Wind thrashed his hair. In the distance, a police helicopter chased a fleeing suspect, its quivering searchlight aimed toward earth.

"You were really good," said Ron, his voice hoarse from Marlboros and tequila. "It'll probably get easier each time you do it." The evening had been for Ron a long bout of vicarious stage fright, and I knew he would think twice before joining us for Bill's next appearance.

In the months that followed, however, such an appearance

looked doubtful. Bill introduced new gags into his act, but he grew sullen and confused as he stood in the living room and honed his delivery. He would sigh, tug at his sweats, curse himself for every slip and miscalculation. Instead of making a joke sharper and funnier, his rehearsal made it labored and stale; he'd forget what it was about the joke that had amused him, had compelled him to tell it in the first place. If he heard an especially good one (What's in the air in San Francisco that prevents pregnancy? Men's legs), he rarely laughed; instead, he picked it apart to see what about its structure or timing made it work. Jokes were like pocket watches: once Bill opened them up and took them apart, he couldn't fit the tiny gears back together, couldn't make them tick again. After his debut at the Comedy Shop, Bill's sense of humor became self-conscious, utilitarian, fraught with anxiety, the success of each joke a test of his professionalism and therefore an omen about his future.

Walking up the flagstone path to his apartment, I was greeted, more and more frequently, with conspicuous silence rather than the patter of a new routine. Often, the only sound and light in the apartment came from the television set. I'd let myself in and find him crumpled on the couch, watching sitcoms, so frustrated he could barely speak. "I've always had a sense of humor," he'd say, "and now I'm losing it." The wryness had gone out of his voice; in its place was a tone more plaintive. His dilemma, I told him, reminded me of the story about the centipede who forgot how to walk because she thought too hard about walking. He had only to relax and his knack would return; this paralysis was temporary. But then I lay beside him on the couch and breathed the acrid scent of a body steeped in its own despair.

Bill ceased to bring with him the notebook he had once taken everywhere, as indispensable as a wallet or house keys. If he did remember to bring it, it stayed tucked in his back pocket or in his gym bag. Ron noticed this one night when we were over at his place for dinner and a few of our clever quips went unrecorded. It was as if the presence of the notebook reminded Bill that his sense of humor had been impaired, that the antics that had once come naturally now led to nothing but effort and doubt. When Bill went into the kitchen for salt, Ron and I commented on his lack of enthusiasm; the person we knew had been obscured and we wanted him back. We agreed to try and talk him into seeing a therapist (a suggestion Bill had recently vetoed for lack of funds). While Vivaldi played in the background, we spooled spaghetti onto our forks and tried to act as if nothing were wrong.

Summer ended. Night fell earlier and earlier. The weather turned cold. Rain stripped the leaves from trees, sent rivers of mud sliding down hillsides. Inhospitable weather could have accounted for Bill's unwillingness to leave his apartment. He kept the windows closed and the drapes drawn. Electric lights burned during the day. The heater blasted a constant gust of suffocating, dusty warmth.

Day by day, the scope of Bill's involvement with the world tightened around him. A jar of ketchup and a few cartons of Chinese take-out were the sole contents of the refrigerator. A mountain of dirty laundry rose from the closet floor. Trips to the supermarket or the Laundromat required him to muster courage, as if he were about to dive into cold water. "What do you do with yourself all day?" I wanted to ask, but I was afraid to add my recriminations to his list of difficulties. Besides, I had a pretty clear picture of Bill's free time: he sat on the couch or lay in bed, the lead of indecision settling into his limbs.

Bill ventured outside only for work. The regularity and obligation of a job was one of the few things that still made sense to him. A few afternoons a week, he filed records for a local dentist. The income from his day job was supplemented by delivering *The Recycler*, a free newspaper, to restaurants and minimarts on Thursday nights. But once the weather turned bad, Bill decided he didn't like driving the company van, claiming the streets were treacherous and slick, the van hard to steer. Suppose he got into an accident, he argued; with his luck he'd have to pay for damages to the van, not to mention his own medical expenses. Quitting his job for *The Recycler* on the grounds of personal safety seemed especially sad to me; Bill once claimed to feel a surge of independence while navigating the streets at night.

Excuses to the dental office required more ingenuity, and Bill had no compunction about lying to his employer in my presence. "That's right," he said into the phone, winking at me, "I've got to pick up my parents at the airport."

Though his parents may have provided a good excuse for missing work, he rarely spoke to them and, as far as I could tell, there was little chance they would ever visit California. Second-generation Arab Americans, Mr. and Mrs. Bader suffered, according to Bill, from a desperate need to fit into the shared life of the small town in Pennsylvania where Mr. Bader ran a stationery store and Mrs. Bader kept house. Forever vigilant about their dress and behavior, Bill's parents were as critical and self-conscious about the impression they made as Bill had become about doing stand-up. The slightest anomaly threatened their sense of belonging. That they reacted with shock and numbness when Bill told them he was gay came as no surprise. Bill liked to do an imitation of them greeting his disclosure by going rigid, smiles frozen, eyes wide, and then thanking him in a monotone for his honesty. The night they learned of their only child's sexual orientation, Mr. and Mrs. Bader announced at dinner that they neither wished to disown him nor know anything more about his "lifestyle"; they expected from him the same discretion he could expect from them, adding that any further discussion of the matter was out of the question, please pass the butter. If he continued to live at home, Bill realized, he'd have to accept conditions his parents considered generous and he considered stifling, conditions that relegated him to a state of limbo between being their son and being himself. He decided to move to Los Angeles, where he hoped to achieve autonomy and fame in a single stroke. And here he was, pinned inside his apartment by depression.

Thinking that physical exercise might lighten Bill's mood, or at least get him out of his house, I prodded him to the Holiday Health Spa several times a week. Just leaving his apartment had become something of a feat. Before he locked the door behind us, Bill would stand in the threshold and balk at the sky: Yes, it was sunny now, but how could he be sure it wouldn't rain later? If he couldn't be certain about the weather, how could he know what clothes to wear? If he decided to bring a jacket, could the jacket be stolen from his locker, or was imagining the possibility of a stolen jacket a sign of instability? Is it true that if you think you're going crazy, chances are, you're not? Contingencies un furled before him. I'd have to take the keys from his hand and lock the door myself.

Working out refreshed Bill, at least temporarily. Exercise had about it a comforting simplicity — so many sets of so many reps, and one's goal was accomplished. After a few minutes of strenuous activity, his breathing grew deep and his head seemed to clear. He even ventured a couple of jokes. Once, while I stood behind the bench press ready to spot him, he looked up and told me my face looked the same upside down as it did right side up, sort of like a playing card. As we moved from machine to machine, the scent of his depression would gradually fade, replaced by a blend of sweat and soap.

Triceps, pectorals, abdomen, calves — his muscles emerged with new definition, as if his body had compensated for his vague, unruly state of mind. Returning home from the gym, Bill examined himself in the medicine cabinet mirror, flexing tentatively, pivoting this way and that. In a hopeful, ingenuous voice, he'd ask me if the improvements he saw were real or a figment of his imagination. To reassure him was to praise his body, and to praise his body was to ring with want. When sex happened, it happened without the preliminaries of lighting or music, without the languorous preamble of foreplay, without a word being spoken, an eyebrow being raised. I'd be reaching for a book or passing him in his hallway and the next thing I knew we'd pounce on each other, trying to start a fire with the friction of our limbs. Sex with Bill was a sudden hungry grappling. It was as if we'd been given twenty minutes to live and found that wrestling naked was the wisest way to spend our time. Bill liked to be clutched and yanked and pounded and slapped. Firm and vigorous sex restored him to senses dulled by despair. When I fucked him, he held on to my shoulders and thrashed beneath me, blathering happy invective. The closer he came to orgasm, the less he writhed, the narrower his focus, till at last, panting with satisfaction, he was gazing into my eyes, perhaps at his own reflection.

Depressed in every other respect, Bill's sex drive flourished, and this alone gave me reason to believe that his unhappiness was a phase. Consumed by my devotion to him, I was only vaguely aware of the possessive nature of that devotion. I wanted to cure Bill of his fragility, and also to prolong it. Taking care of him gave me what I'd always dreamed of: the company of a loyal, handsome man. Bill offered me a steady supply of sex, and what's more, the heady suggestion that sex with me was not just good but therapeutic. In bed with Bill, I felt necessary and potent. The act I'd been led all my life to believe was disgraceful — sex between men — had taken on a curative aspect. A kind of ruthless joy overtook me. If I had to become complicit in a lie to his employer, if I had to do his laundry or bring him Chinese food, if we were locked in an airless intimacy — so be it. Calling my doggedness love, I was willing to put up with almost any problem. Until late one Saturday night.

It had rained all day. Sheets of water cascaded down awnings, clotted the mesh of window screens. When there came a lull in the weather, it was a lull of suspicious, crystalline silence. Just as I grew accustomed to the quiet, rain began to batter the roof. Bill and I had gone to bed early. For the past few weeks, twitching muscles and uneasy dreams had troubled his sleep. I often awoke to the sound of his voice and felt his spasms ripple through the mattress. That night I turned and watched him twist in the blankets, his lips glistening with the spittle of vague but urgent words. No sooner had I caught some fragment of language than I'd wonder if the meaning I'd heard was Bill's, or a meaning I'd gleaned from his gibberish. We shared a threadbare, restive night.

Unable to fall back asleep, I got up, groped through the dark, and poured a glass of water in the kitchen. Stepping back into the bedroom, I heard the first hard drops of a deluge and was blinded when Bill turned on the lamp. When my eyes adjusted, I saw him sitting up, pressed against the headboard. He looked at me, then at my empty place in the bed. Back and forth, back and forth, my presence in the doorway and my vacancy beside him, two dead facts that wouldn't add up. "It's me," I blurted, thinking he might have mistaken me for an intruder. No one I had ever known had stared at me like that, without so much as a shred of recognition, his gaze a kind of erasure. "Bill," I said again, but this time with such force that water sloshed from the glass I'd forgotten in my hand.

"What's that?" he asked, breathing hard.

"A glass of water."

"Did I ask for it? I don't think I remember doing that."

"No. I was thirsty. I got it for myself." I held out the glass, proof that things were what they seemed, but my hand was shaking.

"I thought there were . . ."

"What?"

"I thought there were two of you," he said, his voice about to break. "That's not possible, is it?" Before I could speak, he held up his hand. "If you say yes, that'll scare me. And if you say no, that'll scare me, too."

I climbed into bed, thinking I'd hold him. But he pressed against the headboard, too wary and embarrassed and jumpy to be touched. "I'm losing it," he whispered. We sat side by side and listened to the rain until, at last, he fell asleep.

At that point in my life, the only person I knew who had gone mad was a boy from the neighborhood where I grew up. One afternoon while his parents were out of the house, he moved every chair and lamp and ashtray a couple of inches away from where it had been. To punish himself for this inexplicable mischief, the boy made a pair of paper horns, taped them to his head, and waited in his room. When his parents returned, they moved through the house as though they were lost; everything straight was slightly askew, and everything familiar, strange.

There was something contagious about Bill's deteriorating view of the world. His behavior called into question the mechanics of conversation, the relationship of cause and effect, the rhythms of working and sleeping and eating. Even when I was busy trying to reason with him, I couldn't help but see what I was doing with a certain skepticism; in the presence of someone who was losing his mind, the power of reason seemed tenuous at best. In his crazy way, Bill was right: given the difference between my sense of reality before I met him and my sense of reality after, there might as well have been two of me. I'd stopped writing, neglected my own apartment in order to spend time with him, was late grading papers for the composition classes I taught at a local college. "Things will get better," I told him that night, but my prediction sounded hollow, the impulse to voice it questionable, the logic in the words about to unravel. I saw us from a great height, two baffled men sitting in bed, bound together by sleeplessness and sex.

"Get him help," Terry advised me the next morning, "and then get out. You have a life of your own, remember?" It was a Sunday, "day of rest," as Bill reminded me from under the covers. "I feel really funny," he said whenever I tried to rouse him, "but not ha-ha funny." I recruited Ron to help me make some phone calls on Bill's behalf; together we might find someone who would see Bill that day on an emergency basis. "Poor Billy," Ron lamented between drags. "I knew he would snap."

Ron located a psychiatrist in Claremont who agreed to see Bill that afternoon. Terry and Ron and I made a pact to foot the bill, at least for the initial visit, having no idea how much it would cost; Ron was so relieved to find someone who would open his offices on a Sunday that he forgot to ask about the fee.

Bill consented, through a fog of exhaustion, to get in my car and let me take him to see a psychiatrist. "That's so nice of you," he said, his tone both sincere and impersonal. I wasn't sure he fully understood what was going on. Limp in the seat beside me, Bill spent the drive gazing toward the horizon where clouds smeared the sky like Rorschach blots. Wet stretches of asphalt gleamed in the sunlight. The five-lane freeway was nearly empty, and the landscape seemed to envelop the car, a lucid but unpeopled dream. My anxiety about Bill's future funneled into the fear that I'd miss the right off-ramp and we'd wander through the suburbs forever.

The doctor's office stood on a shady corner near the Claremont foothills, the massive, black-boughed trees around it dripping from the recent rainfall. Spotting the right street number above the glass door, I careened into a parking place on the empty road. "This guy is an expert," I assured Bill, yanking on the parking brake. "He's going to ask a lot of questions. That way, if you need medication, he'll know the right one to give you."

Bill sighed and ran his fingers through his hair. "I didn't even take a shower," he said.

We hardly had time to make ourselves comfortable in the waiting room before the doctor, a tall Japanese man with a tweed jacket and tennis shoes, opened a door and walked into the room. He introduced himself, shook both our hands, and spoke in a calm, inclusive way that acknowledged, without a trace of judgment, my relationship with Bill. Had Ron forewarned him? Was he one of us? It may have been a projection on my part, but I was certain Bill was sobered by the appearance of a total stranger in the long, reclusive drama of his mental collapse. As he entered the consultation room, Bill turned and shot me a somber look. I was relieved to see in his expression an alertness to circumstance and a dread that might motivate change.

For the next forty-five minutes I thumbed through old issues of *Time* and *Life*. As far as I knew, the three of us were the only occupants of the building. Once in a while, I could hear Bill responding to questions, but it was mostly a broken mumbling, like the words he spoke in his sleep. Through a frosted-glass window, the shapes of trees swayed in the wind. Light flickered over the furniture and walls. I tugged from a bookshelf *Physicians' Desk Reference*, a blue doorstop of a book that contained not only the symptomology of every physical and mental condition known to man, but the proper drugs with which to treat them and descriptions of their side effects. A glossy section contained color photographs of hundreds of drugs — Placidyl, Cylert, Tranxene, Lithobid — a confetti of medication.

"I'm suffering from an agitated depression," Bill announced on our way back to the car. Having a name for his state of mind was help in itself. As we accelerated onto the freeway, he pulled from his pocket a foil-wrapped sample of Elavil tablets, which he was to start taking immediately, as well as a prescription for more. The doctor had told him it might take as long as three weeks before the drug brought his mood swings under control. In the meantime, Bill had promised to phone Dr. Arakawa every two or three days, to see him in person once a week, and to go in for tests every few months in order to monitor the drug's effect on his liver and blood chemistry. Dry mouth and dizziness were two of Elavil's possible side effects, but the doctor said that to warn him of further side effects might actually induce them, given Bill's degree of suggestibility. I could feel Bill's mounting agitation as he related, in candid detail, the questions he'd been asked and the answers he'd given. I listened for a while, then stopped him to say that, although I was probably the only other person besides the doctor who could boast a legitimate interest in his dreams and libido and bowel movements, these were matters he would be better off sharing solely with Dr. Arakawa. "I can be your friend," I said, "but I can't be your shrink." It felt liberating to draw this line between us, the first in a series that would lead to our eventual uncoupling. Bill accepted the limits of my involvement with a nod. He gazed at ranks of passing clouds.

Eager to start his regimen, he needed to wash down the pills with something wet. Because they didn't have Orange Julius in Pennsylvania, and because Bill had wanted to taste one ever since he moved to Los Angeles, I careened off the freeway when we saw the sign hovering above the vast expanse of tract houses, strip malls, and prefabricated storage units. It was good to see him register enthusiasm at the prospect of tasting something new. He waited in the car, two Elavil tablets coddled in his palm, while I ordered a couple of large Juliuses. "What is that stuff?" I asked the girl behind the counter as she spooned a few mounds of powder into a cup of orange juice. "We're not allowed to tell," she said, dutiful and curt. The blender roared, the air around the concession stand fragrant with a fine talcum of secret ingredients.

I handed the first Orange Julius to Bill through the passenger window, squeezed his shoulder, and went back for the second.

When I turned to check on him, he raised his paper cup in a toast and smiled tentatively from within the dim interior of the car. He shook the pills like a pair of dice, tossed them into his mouth, and swallowed.

*

A decade later, Martina, the actress from the screening of *The Candle,* called to tell me that Terry had been admitted to Cedars-Sinai in the morning and had died that night. Her feeble, inflectionless voice made me wonder if she'd been sedated. Then her message detonated and left me breathless. "What?" I kept gasping into the mouthpiece. As if at fault for bearing bad news, Martina apologized in her cottony voice.

I'd rarely seen Terry Cahalan during the past few years, though we tried to keep tabs on each other over the phone. He took job after job doctoring scripts that had been optioned for large sums of money but which, after several drafts by the original writer, were still unacceptable to studio executives. Although he hated the requisite car crashes and happy endings, Terry worked on rewrites day and night, hoping to save enough money for a long hiatus. During our last conversation, Terry told me he'd made copious notes for a script he wanted to write, and I recognized the plot from one of our nighttime rides in Ron's convertible. He complained that he'd be able to get more written if his life weren't complicated by an increasing sensitivity to foods. Shrimp, nuts, and wheat had begun to cause rashes. "It's embarrassing," he said, and laughed. "I have to wear long sleeves and sweatpants when I work out. What's the point of busting your ass if you can't show it off?" Terry's doctor was stumped but remained confident that his allergic reactions had nothing to do with AIDS; the test, he thought, was unnecessary, at least for now. I must have echoed the doctor's opinion in my eagerness to allay Terry's fears, and therefore my own.

Martina held a memorial service at her apartment, a gathering of stunned and hesitant strangers. People from the film industry attended, a few of Terry's former teachers and classmates, and two bodybuilders who strained the seams of their pinstriped suits. Though Martina's eyes were red and puffy, she was perfectly coiffed and made up, protected by the soft armor of a sedative. She patted everyone who walked through the door and repeated, as though the irony of it had just struck her, "He was practically a kid, for Christ's sake. Even my grandmothers are still alive." Guests sat around the perimeter of the room on folding chairs and, at Martina's urging, offered anecdotes about Terry. One of the bodybuilders praised Terry's strength at the gym, then stared into his massive lap and said he couldn't think of more to say. A teacher from film school recounted an argument they'd had about the computer-generated films of the 1960s, which Terry insisted were spiritually bankrupt despite all those mandalas undulating to sitar music. Sure he was a hulk, remarked the woman who had typed his scripts, but she would always remember his extraordinary vulnerability; she even thought it grimly fitting that he should die from a disease that would make him susceptible to every organism out there. I found it difficult to listen to the other guests. Some of them described versions of Terry I didn't recognize, which made him seem unknowable. I blamed myself for not visiting him more often and cursed the circumstances that allow people to drift apart. While the others spoke, I mined the past for a charm against forgetting. When it came my turn to speak, I described how Terry fitfully modeled T-shirts before we went out on the town, and what I envisioned, more clearly than I'd ever envision it again, was my friend's pale torso naked to the waist. The eulogies continued for half an hour. In the silences between them, we peered into the empty center of the room.

Not long after the memorial service at Martina's apartment, I received a phone call from Bill Bader's lover, Andy, telling me that Bill was dead. The last time Ron and I had seen them was almost two years earlier, at a party they'd thrown to show off improvements on their clapboard bungalow in Santa Monica.

Since then, said Andy, the virus played havoc with the mental stability it had taken Bill so long to achieve. Early in the progress of the disease, Bill found that he bruised easily. This was before he'd taken the test, and he wasn't sure whether he was only imagining this symptom, or whether it warranted his genuine concern. According to Andy, Bill had become so alarmed about his propensity to bruise, he purposely struck his arm on the edge of a Formica counter they were installing in their kitchen. Bill studied his skin for the rest of the day, apprehensive, mesmerized. Every few minutes he held his arm up to the light, tested its sensitivity to pressure. When a bruise finally did appear, Bill still couldn't decide if the tender, darkening flesh was a normal or an abnormal reaction to the self-inflicted blow. He threatened to strike himself again, but Andy talked him out of it. Bill resisted Andy's suggestion that he see a physician, saying he was practically a walking pharmacy already, filled with enough Elavil to tranquilize an elephant. And besides, he added, it would scare him to death to find out he had a fatal disease. The more Andy insisted he seek a doctor's opinion, the more Bill blamed his problems on hypochondria. Mental infirmities were familiar to Bill, and less frightening than physical illness. How was it possible to argue with him, Andy had protested, when half the gay men in America *were* turning into hypochondriacs, every ache or pain the beginning of the end. And so Bill continued to worry, to doubt his body, to scrutinize every inch of himself till he no longer knew what his own flesh meant. Andy would discover him in the bedroom, furtively tugging up his sleeves or pulling down his pants to see if any bruises had appeared since the last time he looked. One night, stripping before the medicine cabinet mirror, he mistook the shadows of his muscles for bruises and Andy's name exploded from his throat. Bill had become a stranger to himself, had "lost it" once again. Embarrassment about his relapse made him secretive and, in the last days of his life, as confused and reclusive as he had been when I first took him to see Dr. Arakawa.

Thinking it might help Bill to hear from his parents, Andy took it upon himself to call Pennsylvania and tell them that Bill had tested positive for the AIDS virus. They phoned Bill immediately but pretended they were making a routine call, determined not to bring up the subject of his health unless he brought it up first. Perhaps they hadn't heard much about AIDS, or had heard about it and thought it was something temporary, exaggerated, a sensational headline with a hint of science fiction. After not having heard from his parents for so long, Bill was afraid to spoil their present conversation and perhaps ruin the possibility of future conversations by discussing his HIV status. And so his health was never discussed. By the time his parents finally made arrangements to fly out to see him, Bill had been admitted to the hospital with toxoplasmosis and had lapsed into a coma. That the Baders never left Bill's side once they arrived made Andy secretly furious; it robbed him of private time with Bill and, as far as the doctors and nurses were concerned, gave the Baders an air of angelic dedication. While staring at his sallow boy, Bill's father gripped the metal railing as if to hold the bed in place. His mother swore Bill squeezed her hand, an ambiguous and mild pressure that would have to last her the rest of her life.

After Bill was pronounced dead, Andy drove Mr. and Mrs. Bader back to the house in Santa Monica. He apologized for the raw wallboard and exposed wiring, and told them a little about the improvements he and Bill were making on the place. Had planned to make. Andy fought back tears as he talked, tears he felt would put him at a disadvantage in his unspoken contest of stoicism with Mr. and Mrs. Bader. Though they tried to be polite, to muster some interest, Bill's parents couldn't hide their discomfort at this evidence of domesticity between two men. That clapboard bungalow made their child's sex life unarguable and stark. The Baders thanked Andy for taking good care of their boy and asked him to call them a cab. Before they left for their hotel, Andy handed them a bundle of Bill's belongings — his wallet and watch, the notebook in which he'd scribbled jokes — packed inside a cardboard box. I imagined Bill's parents, weary and bewildered, eyeing the box as if to say, You've made a mistake. This is not our son. These are only his things.

I phoned Ron the instant after I hung up with Andy. "Bill," said Ron with eerie calm, as if to feel the shape of his name. The rasp of a match. A long exhalation. Ron believed that psychotropic drugs had weakened Bill's immune system, and this, combined with a sex drive that even heavy doses of Elavil and a steady boyfriend couldn't dampen, had probably caused him to contract AIDS. In the early days of the epidemic, it was important for Ron and me to try and pinpoint the set of circumstances, the turns of luck, or the simple, unwitting errors in judgment that might have provided a path of transmission. Reasons seemed to dull the blow — until the next unreasonable death.

During this time I belonged to Weight-Lifter's gym. I'd been a member ever since I'd broken up with Bill and moved to East Hollywood. The condition of Weight-Lifter's had declined rapidly since Bobby's death from AIDS. Never cleaned, the mirrors grew streaked and grimy. When examining their abs or flexing their triceps, members were confronted with a hazy reflection, like a body remembered rather than seen. Clocks stopped running. Fans stopped turning. Mildew filmed the shower doors.

Listless, quiet, mired in sorrow, Ted made occasional attempts to improve the place, but even his improvements — mismatched swatches of paint on the walls, leather seats patched with electrical tape — made the gym's demise more apparent. Dank, neglected, in constant disrepair, Weight-Lifter's became a monument to mourning.

Following Bobby's funeral, Ted himself began to show signs of illness — weight loss, cough, a low-grade fever — and all of us wondered whether he too was infected, or simply worn out by weeks of despair. Ted's love for Bobby had been as tenacious as it was indulgent, and I couldn't help but suspect that Ted had manifested these symptoms as a form of sympathy for his former lover. Could sickness be a vestige of devotion? Could one man's fever continue in another, passed on like a torch?

As for the rest of us at Weight-Lifter's, the physiques we tried to strengthen and perfect became increasingly alien to us, capable of every failure and betrayal. More and more often, we turned toward the mirrors to examine our skin for lesions and our mouths for thrush, and we did so as unabashedly as we had once examined our limbs for definition, except that pride was replaced by panic. And then the big blond lawyer disappeared. And the lanky carpenter nicknamed Driftwood. The friendly incessant whistler. The limber old man who counted aloud. The boy whose back was tattooed with aircraft. Maybe they went to other gyms. Maybe they moved to different cities. Maybe they died in the night. One day someone awoke with a sore neck and the next with meningitis. Someone bit his tongue and it wouldn't stop bleeding. Blindness, dementia, paralysis. Anything could happen. Anyone might vanish. Fate took sudden, improbable turns, all of them unjust. One man, despite all the evidence to the contrary, was afraid to drink from the water fountain at Weight-Lifter's. Another wanted to tempt the disease he'd grown to hate for robbing him of friends, and bragged about fucking himself to death. Ever since I'd heard about "gay cancer," I worried that it incubated inside me. The test was new, and I was too afraid to take it; I bore my health like a delicate bubble, and imagined my death again and again. *Zinc, acupuncture, seaweed, might stop it. The test is unreliable. A quarantine is imminent.* Rumors multiplied like viruses. The gym became a source of hearsay and news, of losses in the face of which all consolation paled.

Ted finally decided this avalanche of grief was too much for him and left town on an indefinite vacation. Most of the responsibilities for running the gym were handed over to Lyle Barker, who had worked at the front desk while Bobby was in the hospital. More mascot than manager, Lyle did little in the way of actually assisting the members, oiling the machines, or keeping the place clean. Short and stocky, animated by his new authority, Lyle strutted around the gym. He'd perch atop the equipment and chat incessantly, stroking his bristly, graying goatee. Besides his theory that AIDS was a government experiment in germ warfare gone awry, Lyle's favorite topic of conversation was Bobby's art. Lyle knew or cared nothing about aesthetics until he'd met Bobby, and since Bobby's was the only art he'd ever thought about, he considered himself an expert and talked about it with the tireless enthusiasm of a museum docent. According to Lyle, this art tackled "major stuff," notions of physical perfection, the planets aligned in "cosmic harmony," landscapes that hinted at a paradise on earth. The idealism in Bobby's art had turned Lyle appreciative, poetic, stirring in him ideas and sensations he claimed never to have known before.

Since Bobby's death, however, the balsa wood models of workout equipment grew fuzzy with dust. Perpetually crooked, the paintings of rainbows and unicorns faded from exposure to sunlight. Drawings of Mr. Olympia contestants curled at the edges from the moisture of the steam room, beads of water trapped behind the glass. Lyle hated seeing Bobby's oeuvre fall to ruin. Being an entrepreneur at heart, and believing art became more valuable following the artist's death, Lyle hatched a plan not only to rescue the work from obscurity, but to make some extra cash on the side.

"I've got it all figured out," said Lyle as I finished a set of crossovers. Lyle often sought my approval in matters of aesthetics because I was the only person he knew at the gym who had studied art history in school. "I may even make Bobby immortal."

"How?" I asked, catching my breath.

Lyle told me to follow him to the parking lot behind the gym. Exercise was one of the only antidotes for my nearly constant anxiety about AIDS, and I was eager to get back inside. During our walk to the lot, Lyle grinned expectantly and tossed his key ring into the air. It was one of those eerie afternoons, bright despite the blanket of haze, as hot in the shade as it was in the sun. Lyle's white Buick glared like an iceberg against the asphalt. He inserted the key, flung open the trunk.

Taking up the entire trunk were hundreds of color reproductions of one of Bobby's paintings. They ranged in size from about a yard to a foot square. The painting was one that I recalled having seen at the gym. Jagged green mountains rose in the background. Beneath them meandered a skinny river, a few white strokes suggesting spume. The landscape was flat and unremarkable, with one surreal exception: in the upper left-hand corner, a man's head rose on an updraft. His eyes were closed, mouth slack, his skin translucent as the skin of a balloon.

Lyle told me how he planned to rent a gallery and advertise an exhibit in art magazines. He'd sunk most of his savings into the scheme, not to mention all of his free time. Lyle admitted he was taking a big gamble, the whims of the art market being hard to second-guess.

Sunlight burned the nape of my neck. The trunk was hot and smelled like rubber. I reached down, sifted through the stacks, saw face after weightless, disembodied face.

Picking Plums

~~~~~~~~~~~~~~~~~~~~~~~

It has been nearly a year since my father fell while picking plums. The bruises on his leg have healed, and except for a vague absence of pigmentation where the calf had blistered, his recovery is complete. Back in the habit of evening constitutionals, he navigates the neighborhood with his usual stride — "Brisk," he says, "for a man of eighty-five" — dressed in a powder blue jogging suit that bears the telltale stains of jelly doughnuts and Lipton's tea, foods which my father, despite doctor's orders, hasn't the will to forsake.

He broke his glasses and his hearing aid in the fall, and when I first stepped into the hospital room for a visit, I was struck by the way my father — head cocked to hear, squinting to see — looked so much older and more remote, a prisoner of his failing senses. "Boychik?" he asked, straining his face in my general direction. He fell back into a stack of pillows, sighed a deep sigh, and without my asking described what had happened:

"There they are, all over the lawn. Purple plums, dozens of them. They look delicious. So what am I supposed to do? Let the birds eat them? Not on your life. It's my tree, right? First I fill a bucket with the ones from the ground. Then I get the ladder out of the garage. I've climbed the thing a hundred times before. I make it to the top, reach out my hand, and . . . who knows what happens. Suddenly I'm an astronaut. Up is down and vice versa.

It happened so fast I didn't have time to piss in my pants. I'm flat on my back, not a breath left in me. Couldn't have called for help if I tried. And the pain in my leg — you don't want to know."

"Who found you?"

"What?"

I move closer, speak louder.

"Nobody found me," he says, exasperated. "Had to wait till I could get up on my own. It seemed like hours. I'm telling you, I thought it was all over. But eventually I could breathe normal again and, don't ask me how, God only knows, I got in the car and drove here myself."

"You should have called me."

"You were probably busy."

"It was an emergency, Dad. What if you hadn't been able to drive?"

"You don't have to shout. I made it here, didn't I?" My father shifted his weight and grimaced. The sheet slid off his injured leg, the calf swollen, purple as a plum, what the doctor called "an insult to the tissue."

*

Throughout my boyhood my father possessed a surplus of energy, or it possessed him. On weekdays he worked hard at the office, and on weekends he gardened in our yard. He was also a man given to unpredictable episodes of anger. These rages were never precipitated by a crisis. In the face of illness or accident my father remained steady, methodical, even optimistic. When the chips were down, he was an incorrigible joker, a sentry at the bedside. But something as simple as a drinking glass left out on the table could send him into a frenzy of invective. Spittle shot from his lips. Blood ruddied his face. He'd hurl the glass against the wall.

His temper rarely intimidated my mother. She'd light a Tareyton, stand aside, and watch my father flail and shout until he was purged of the last sharp word. Winded and limp, he'd flee into the living room, where he would draw the shades, sit in his wing chair, and brood for hours. Mother got out the broom and the dustpan and — presto! — the damage disappeared. Shards of glass slid into the trash can, chimed against the metal sides. And when Mother lifted her foot from the pedal and the lid fell shut with a thud, I knew the ordeal was over.

Even as a boy, I understood how my father's profession had sullied his view of the world, had made him a wary man, prone to explosions. He spent hours taking depositions from jilted wives and cuckolded husbands. He conferred with a miserable clientele: spouses who wept, who spat accusations, who pounded his desk in want of revenge. At this time, California law required that grounds for divorce be proven in court, and toward this end my father carried in his briefcase not only the usual legal tablets and manila files but bills for motel rooms, matchbooks from bars, boxer shorts blooming with lipstick stains. It was his job to exploit every detail of an infidelity, to unearth the most tawdry and incontrovertible evidence of betrayal. Year in and year out, my father met with a steady parade of strangers and itemized insults, blows, deceits.

After one particularly long and vindictive divorce trial, he agreed to a weekend out of town. Mother suggested Palm Springs, rhapsodized about the balmy air, the cacti lit by colored lights, the street named after Bob Hope. When it finally came time to leave, however, my mother kept thinking of things she'd forgotten to pack. No sooner would my father begin to back the car out of the driveway than my mother would shout for him to stop, dash into the house, and retrieve what she needed. A carton of Tareytons. An aerosol can of Solarcaine. A paperback novel to read by the pool. I sat in the back seat, motionless and mute; with each of her excursions back inside, I felt my father's frustration mount. When my mother insisted she get a package of Saltine crackers in case we got hungry along the way, my father glared at her, bolted from the car, wrenched every piece of luggage from the trunk, and slammed it shut with such a vengeance the car rocked on its springs. Through the rear window, my mother and I could see him fling two suitcases, a carryall, and a make-up case yards above his balding head. The sky was a huge and cloudless blue; gray chunks of luggage sailed through it, twisting and spinning and falling to earth like the burnt-out stages of a booster rocket. When a piece of luggage crashed back to the asphalt, he'd pick it up and hurl it again.

Mother and I got out of the car and sat together on a low wall by the side of the driveway, waiting for his tantrum to pass. "Some vacation," she said, lighting a cigarette. Her cheeks imploded from the vigorous draw. In order to watch him, we had to shield our eyes against the sun, a light so stark it made me want to sneeze. Sometimes my father managed to launch two or three pieces of luggage into the air at the same time. With every effort, an involuntary, animal grunt issued from the depths of his chest. Once or twice, a suitcase flew up and eclipsed the sun, and I remember thinking how small and aloof it really was, not like the fat and friendly star my classmates drew in school.

Finally, the largest suitcase came unlatched in mid-flight. Even my father was astonished when articles of his wife's wardrobe began their descent from the summer sky. A yellow scarf dazzled the air like a tangible strand of sunlight. Fuzzy slippers tumbled down. One diaphanous white slip drifted over the driveway and, as if guided by an invisible hand, draped itself across a hedge. With that, my father barreled by us, veins protruding on his temple and neck, and stomped into the house. "I'm getting tired of this," my mother grumbled. Before she stooped to pick up the mess — a vast and random geography of clothes — she flicked her cigarette onto the asphalt and ground out the ember.

*

One evening, long after I'd moved away from home, I received a phone call from my father telling me that my mother had died the night before. "But I didn't know it happened," he said.

He'd awakened as usual that morning, ruminating over a case while he showered and shaved. My mother appeared to be sound asleep, one arm draped across her face, eyes sheltered beneath the crook of her elbow. When he sat on the bed to pull up his socks he'd tried not to jar the mattress and wake her. At least he thought he'd tried not to wake her, but he couldn't remember, he couldn't be sure. Things looked normal, he kept protesting — the pillow, the blanket, the way she lay there. He decided to grab a doughnut downtown and left in a hurry. But that night my father returned to a house suspiciously unlived-in. The silence caused him to clench his fists, and he called for his wife, "Lillian, Lillian," as he drifted through quiet, unlit rooms, walking slowly up the stairs.

I once saw a photograph of a woman who had jumped off the Empire State Building and landed on the roof of a parked car. What is amazing is that she appeared merely to have leapt into satin sheets. Deep in a languid and absolute sleep, her eyes are closed, lips slightly parted, hair fanned out on a metal pillow. Nowhere is there a trace of blood, her body caught softly in its own impression.

As my father spoke into the telephone, his voice about to break — "I should have realized, I should have known" — that's the state in which I pictured my mother: a long fall of sixty years, an uncanny landing, a miraculous repose.

*

My father and I had one thing in common after my mother's heart attack: we each maintained a secret life. Secret, at least, from each other.

I'd fallen for a man named Travis Mask. Travis had recently arrived in Los Angeles from Kentucky, and everything I was accustomed to — the billboards lining the Sunset Strip, the 7-Elevens open all night — stirred in him a strong allegiance. "I love this town," he'd say every day. Travis's job was to collect change from vending machines throughout the city. During dinner he would tell me about the office lobbies and college cafeterias he had visited, the trick to opening different machines, the noisy cascade of nickels and dimes. Travis Mask was enthusiastic. Travis Mask was easy to please. In bed I called him by his full name because I found the sound of it exciting.

And my father had fallen for a woman whose identity he meant to keep secret. I knew of her existence only because of a dramatic change in his behavior: he would grow mysterious as quickly and inexplicably as he had once grown angry. Ordinary conversations would take confusing turns. One night I phoned him at home and tried to make a date for dinner.

"Sounds good," he said. "How about next. . . ." A voice in the background interrupted. "As I was saying," he continued, "I'll have the papers for you by Friday."

"OK," I said stupidly. "What papers?"

"It's no problem at all."

"Dad, what's going on?"

"We'll have to have them countersigned, of course."

"Let me guess. You have company."

"No," he said. "Thank *you*."

After he hung up, I began to wonder why my father couldn't simply admit that he had a girlfriend. I'd told him on several occasions that I hoped he could find companionship, that I knew he must be lonely without my mother. What did he have to gain by keeping his relationship a secret? Or was it *my* existence he was trying to hide from her? I'd gone back to watching the evening news with Travis when an awful thought occurred to me. Suppose a robber had forced his way into my father's house, pointed a gun at his head, and ordered him to continue talking as if nothing had happened. What if our officious conversation had really been a signal for help? I tried to remember every word, every inflection. Hadn't there been an unnatural tension in his voice, a strain I'd never heard before? I dismissed this thought as preposterous, only to have it boomerang back. Nearly an hour passed before I decided to call him again. Six rings. Seven. His voice was dreamy, expansive, when he answered, his hello as round and buoyant as a bubble. I hung up without speaking, and when I told Travis I was upset because my father refused to be frank, he said, "Honey, you're a hypocrite."

Travis was right, of course. I resented being barred from this central fact of my father's life but had no intention of telling him I was gay. It had taken me thirty years to achieve even a modicum of intimacy with the man, and I didn't want to risk a setback. It wasn't as if I was keeping my sexual orientation a secret from everyone; I'd told relatives, coworkers, friends. But my father was a man who whistled at waitresses, flirted with bank tellers, his head swiveling like a radar dish toward the nearest pair of breasts and hips. Ever since I was a child my father reminded me of the cartoon wolf whose ears shoot steam, whose eyes pop out on springs, whose tongue unfurls like a party favor whenever he sees a curvaceous dame. As far as my father was concerned, desire for women fueled the world, compelled every man without exception (his occupation testified to that), was a force as essential as gravity. I didn't want to disappoint him.

Eventually, Travis Mask's company transferred him to Long Beach. In his absence, my nights grew long and ponderous, and I tried to spend more time with my father in the belief that sooner or later an opportunity for disclosure would present itself. We met for dinner once a month in a restaurant whose interior was dim and crimson, our interaction friendly but formal, both of us cautiously skirting the topic of our private lives; we'd become expert at the ambiguous answer, the changed subject, the half-truth. Should my father ask if I was dating, I'd tell him yes, I had been seeing someone. I'd liked them very much, I said, but they were transferred to another city. Them. They. My attempt to neuter the pronouns made it sound as if I were courting people en masse. Just when I thought this subterfuge was becoming obvious, my father began to respond in kind. "Too bad I didn't get a chance to meet them. Where did you say they went?"

Avoidance also worked in reverse: "And how about you, Dad? Are you seeing anybody?"

"Seeing? I don't know if you'd call it *seeing*. What did you order, chicken or fish?"

It may seem as if this phase of our relationship was in some way an unhappy accommodation, but I enjoyed visiting with my father during that period and even found it challenging to find things to talk about. During one dinner we discovered that we shared a fondness for nature programs on television, and from that night on, when we'd exhausted our comments about the meal or the weather, we'd ask if the other had seen the show about the blind albino fish that live in underwater caves, or the one about the North American moose, whose antlers, coated with green moss, provide camouflage in the underbrush. My father and I had adapted like those creatures to the strictures of our shared world.

And then I met her.

I looked up from a rack of stationery at the local Thrifty one afternoon and there stood my father with a willowy black woman in her early forties. As she waited for a prescription to be filled, he drew a finger through her hair, nuzzled the nape of her neck, the refracted light of his lenses causing his cheeks to glow. I felt like a child who was witness to something forbidden: his father's helpless, unguarded ardor for an unfamiliar woman. I didn't know whether to run or stay. Had he always been attracted to young black women? Had I ever known him well? Somehow I managed to move myself toward them and mumble hello. They turned around in unison. My father's eyes widened. He reached out and cupped my shoulder, struggled to say my name. Before he could think to introduce us, I shook the woman's hand, startled by its softness. "So you're the son. Where've you been hiding?" She was kind and cordial, though too preoccupied to engage in much conversation, her handsome features furrowed by a hint of melancholy, a sadness that I sensed had little to do with my surprise appearance. Anna excused herself when the pharmacist called her name.

Hours after our encounter, I could still feel the softness of Anna's hand, the softness that stirred my father's yearning. He was seventy-five years old, myopic and hard of hearing, his skin loose and liver-spotted, but one glimpse of his impulsive public affection led me to the conclusion that my father possessed, despite his age, a restless sexual energy. The meeting left me elated, expectant. My father and I had something new in common: the pursuit of our unorthodox passions. We were, perhaps, more alike than I'd realized. After years of relative estrangement, I'd been given grounds for a fresh start, a chance to establish a stronger connection. The final hurdle, however, involved telling my father I was gay, and now there was Anna's reaction to consider. But none of my expectations mattered. Later that week, they left the country.

*

The prescription, it turned out, was for a psychotropic drug. Anna had battled bouts of depression since childhood. Her propensity for unhappiness gave my father a vital mission: to make her laugh, to wrest her from despair. Anna worked as an elementary school substitute teacher and managed a few rental properties in South Central Los Angeles, but after weeks of functioning normally, she would take to my father's bed for days on end, blank and immobile beneath the quilt she had bought to brighten up the room, unaffected by his jokes, his kisses and cajoling. These spells of depression came without warning and ended just as unexpectedly. Though they both did their best to enjoy each other during the periods of relative calm, they lived, my father lamented later, like people in a thunderstorm, never knowing when lightning would strike. Thinking that a drastic change might help Anna shed a recent depression, they pooled their money and flew to Europe.

They returned with snapshots showing the two of them against innumerable backdrops. The Tower of London, the Vatican, Versailles. Monuments, obelisks, statuary. In every pose their faces were unchanged, the faces of people who want to be happy, who try to be happy, and somehow can't.

As if in defiance of all the photographic evidence against them, they were married the following month at the Church of the Holy Trinity. I was one of only two guests at the wedding. The other was an uncle of Anna's. Before the ceremony began, he shot me a glance which attested, I was certain, to an incredulity as great as mine. The vaulted chapel rang with prerecorded organ music, an eerie and pious overture. Light filtered through stained glass windows, chunks of sweet color that reminded me of Jell-O. My old Jewish father and his Episcopalian lover appeared at opposite ends of the dais, walking step by measured step toward a union in the center. The priest, swimming in white vestments, was somber and almost inaudible. Cryptic gestures, odd props; I watched with a powerful, wordless amazement. Afterward, as if the actual wedding hadn't been surreal enough, my father and Anna formed a kind of receiving line (if two people can constitute a line) in the church parking lot, where the four of us, bathed by hazy sunlight, exchanged pleasantries before the newlyweds returned home for a nap; their honeymoon in Europe, my father joked, had put the cart before the horse.

During the months after the wedding, when I called my father, he answered as though the ringing of the phone had been an affront. When I asked him what was the matter, he'd bark, "What makes you think there's something the matter?" I began to suspect that my father's frustration had given rise to those ancient rages. But my father had grown too old and frail to sustain his anger for long. When we saw each other — Anna was always visiting relatives or too busy or tired to join us — he looked worn, embattled, and the pride I had in him for attempting an interracial marriage, for risking condemnation in the eyes of the world, was overwhelmed now by concern. He had lost weight. His hands began to shake. I would sit across from him in the dim red restaurant and marvel that this bewildered man had once hurled glasses against a wall and launched Samsonite into the sky.

Between courses, I'd try to distract my father from his problems by pressing him to unearth tidbits of his past, as many as memory would allow. He'd often talk about Atlantic City, where his parents had owned a small grocery. Sometimes my mother turned up in the midst of his sketchy regressions. He would smooth wrinkles from the tablecloth and tell me no one could take her place. He eulogized her loyalty and patience, and I wondered whether he could see her clearly — her auburn hair and freckled hands — wondered whether he wished she were here to sweep up after his current mess. "Remember," he once asked me, without a hint of irony or regret, "what fun we had in Palm Springs?" Then he snapped back into the present and asked what was taking so long with our steaks.

*

The final rift between my father and Anna must have come abruptly; she left behind several of her possessions, including the picture of Jesus that sat on the sideboard in the dining room next to my father's brass menorah. And along with Anna's possessions were stacks of leather-bound books, *Law of Torts*, *California Jurisprudence*, and *Forms of Pleading and Practice* embossed on their spines. Too weak and distracted to practice law, my father had retired, and the house became a repository for the contents of his former office. I worried about him being alone, wandering through rooms freighted with history, crowded with the evidence of two marriages, fatherhood, and a long and harrowing career; he had nothing to do but pace and sigh and stir up dust. I encouraged him to find a therapist, but as far as my father was concerned, psychiatrists were all conniving witch doctors who fed off the misery of people like Anna.

Brian, the psychotherapist I'd been living with for three years, was not at all fazed by my father's aversion to his profession. They'd met only rarely (once we ran into my father at a local supermarket, and twice Brian accompanied us to the restaurant), but when they were together, Brian would draw my father out, compliment him on his plaid pants, ask questions regarding the fine points of law. And when my father spoke, Brian listened intently, embraced him with his cool blue gaze. If the subject of Brian's occupation arose, my father seemed secretly delighted to learn that there were so many people in the world burdened with grim and persistent problems, people worse off than either he or Anna. My father relished my lover's attention; Brian's cheerfulness and steady disposition must have been refreshing in those troubled, lonely days. "How's that interesting friend of yours?"

he sometimes asked. If he suspected that Brian and I shared the same house, he never pursued it. Over the years my father and I had come to the tacit understanding that I would never marry, and instead of expressing alarm or asking why, I'm afraid he simply assumed that the problematic examples of his own marriages had made me a skeptic when it came to romance and therefore a confirmed bachelor. And if my father did understand, consciously or subconsciously, that Brian and I were in love, I liked to believe he was happy I ended up with someone sane and solvent — a witch doctor, yes, but a doctor nevertheless. My father, in short, never seemed compelled to inquire about the particulars of my life (it was enough to know I was healthy and happy) until he took his fall from the plum tree.

*

I drove my father home from the hospital, tried to keep his big unwieldy car, bobbing like a boat, within the lane. I bought my father a pair of seersucker shorts because long pants were too painful and constricting. I brought over groceries and my wok, and while I cooked dinner he sat at the dinette table, leg propped on a vinyl chair, and listened to the hissing oil, happy, abstracted. I helped him up the stairs to his bedroom, where we watched "Wheel of Fortune" and "Jeopardy!" on television and where, for the first time since I was a boy, I sat at his feet and he rubbed my head. It felt so good that I grazed his good leg, as contented as a cat. He welcomed my visits with an eagerness bordering on glee, and didn't seem to mind being dependent on me for physical assistance; he leaned his bulk on my shoulder wholly, and I felt protective, necessary, inhaling the scents of salve and Old Spice, and the base, familiar odor that was all my father's own.

*

"You know those hostages?" asked my father. He was sitting at the dinette, dressed in the seersucker shorts, his leg propped on the chair. The bruises had faded to lavender, his calf back to its normal size.

I could barely hear him over the broccoli sizzling in the wok. "What about them?" I shouted.

"I heard on the news that some of them are seeing a psychiatrist now that they're back."

"So?"

"Why a psychiatrist?"

I stopped tossing the broccoli. "Dad," I said, "if you'd been held hostage in the Middle East, you might want to see a therapist, too."

The sky dimmed in the kitchen windows. My father's face was a silhouette, his lenses catching the last of the light. "They got their food taken care of, right? And a place to sleep. What's the big deal?"

"You're at gunpoint, for God's sake. A prisoner. I don't think it's like spending a weekend at the Hilton."

"Living alone," he said matter-of-factly, "is like being a prisoner."

I let it stand. I added the pea pods.

"Let me ask you something," said my father. "I get this feeling — I'm not sure how to say it — that something isn't right. That you're keeping something from me. We don't talk much, I grant you that. But maybe now's the time."

My heart was pounding. I'd been thoroughly disarmed by his interpretation of world events, his minefield of non sequiturs, and I wasn't prepared for a serious discussion. I switched off the gas. The red jet sputtered. When I turned around, my father was staring at his outstretched leg. "So?" he said.

"You mean Brian?"

"Whatever you want to tell me, tell me."

"You like him, don't you?"

"What's not to like."

"He's been my lover for a long time. He makes me happy. We have a home." Each declaration was a stone in my throat. "I hope you understand. I hope this doesn't come between us."

"Look," said my father without skipping a beat, "you're lucky to have someone. And he's lucky to have you, too. It's no one's business anyway. What the hell else am I going to say?"

But my father thought of something else before I could speak and express my relief. "You know," he said, "when I was a boy, maybe sixteen, my father asked me to hold a ladder while he trimmed the tree in our backyard. So I did, see, when I suddenly remember I have a date with this bee-yoo-tiful girl, and I'm late, and I run out of the yard. I don't know what got into me. I'm halfway down the street when I remember my father, and I think, Oh, boy. I'm in trouble now. But when I get back I can hear him laughing way up in the tree. I'd never heard him laugh like that. 'You must like her a lot,' he says when I help him down. Funny thing was, I hadn't told him where I was going."

I pictured my father's father teetering above the earth, a man hugging the trunk of a tree and watching his son run down the street in pursuit of sweet, ineffable pleasure. While my father reminisced, night obscured the branches of the plum tree, the driveway where my mother's clothes once floated down like enormous leaves. When my father finished telling the story, he looked at me, then looked away. A moment of silence lodged between us, an old and obstinate silence. I wondered whether nothing or everything would change. I spooned our food onto separate plates. My father carefully pressed his leg to test the healing flesh.

Train of Thought

I searched through *Brewer's Dictionary of Phrase and Fable* to find information on the expression *train of thought*, but found nothing under either *train* or *thought*. Certainly the origin of that expression couldn't have predated the invention of the locomotive in 1801. Before 1801, when a person was alert to a clattering onslaught of thoughts, big overloaded boxcars of thought, thoughts linked together and barreling by, what expression would that person have used? Take Voltaire, for instance, who was reputed to write while consuming more than thirty cups of coffee a day. (No wonder Candide endures misfortunes from pratfall to flogging in a mere ninety pages.) Perhaps Voltaire, pen ashudder, likened his thoughts to stampeding horses or a swarm of bees. Had there been trains in the 1700s, it's not impossible that Voltaire himself would have been the one to coin the phrase *train of thought*, though *coin* is far too sluggish a verb to describe how that metaphor would have heaved itself upon him, careened through his imagination, preceded and followed by a dozen thoughts of equal interest, as he paced the dining car, coffee cup in hand, Parisian townships surging past the window, blurred as drops of gouache in water.

The etymology of this expression stems from the industrial age, that reign of clanking mechanical contraptions, pistons pumping, conveyor belts conveying. But it's a sadly lacking expression for the post–industrial age, when voluminous amounts of information are flicked across continents in nanoseconds and practically every week physicists proclaim the existence of a sub-atomic particle that is smaller and shorter-lived and more elusive than the particle thought to be the fundamental building block of matter the day before. And what with frequent technological advances in the rapid transmission of words and images, from telex to modem to satellite dish, even the *lightning* in the term *lightning fast* seems feeble and inadequate, a waning glow in our vocabulary.

So the question is how to update the phrase *train of thought*, how to dust it off, streamline its antiquated angles, how to make it purr like a monorail, swoop through the beleaguered imagination with the thrust of the Concorde surpassing sound. You can replace the cowcatcher with a nose cone, use plutonium instead of coal, fit the caboose with a booster rocket, but that won't make it modern for long. At the rate science proceeds, rockets and missiles may one day seem like buffalo — slow, endangered grazers in the black pasture of outer space.

It was only thirty years ago that my father read me asleep from *The Big Book of Trains.* Each illustrated page explained the function of a single car — hopper, tank, flatcar, stock car — and I'd pull away from the station of my waking toward the deep, improbable twilight of dreams. In the realm of dreams there was a train of thought too, but wheeling freely off its track, strange fumes spewing from the smokestack. In one seminal dream from my childhood I was on a train with a woman who was dressed in an enormous satin skirt. I was sitting on her lap and we ladled cupfuls of cool water into each other's mouths. Her petticoats crackled whenever I lifted the cup to her lips. "Where are we going?" I asked her. "To the city," she said, "where the rustling of a woman's skirt sounds the same as the rain." I remember that dream because it was the first dream from which I awoke with a phrase intact, a phrase that withstood the morning light, and I fell in love with words.

Watching TV when I was ten, I saw a lengthy succession of freight rolling past a boy my age. After it passed, he recited for a reporter the serial number and product name printed on the side of each car: Alpine Timber, 56782; Dromedary Products, 92301; Bandy Brothers Cattle, 94933. I envied the reach and precision of his memory, even after I learned that the boy was an "idiot savant," incapable of tying his shoelaces or naming the country in which he lived. I wonder, would it be so bad to be stunted in the face of ordinary tasks if one, just one train in your entire life, rumbled by and scored your mind with its indelible impression, its manifold numbers and assonant names, its raucous livestock, ripe oranges, mounds of ore, its pattern of sunlight bursting through the slats?

So many streets in downtown Los Angeles are embedded with unused railroad track. On rainy days, they gleam like the trail a snail leaves, veering off, aimless tangents, miles of metal sunk in puddles. Perhaps if you viewed them from the fortieth floor of the new Conoco Corporation headquarters, they would form the letters of a brief lament, a poem composed of cursive rails, about history washed away by rain, about the city's relentless change, the wrecking balls, boarded windows, haunted train yards, extinct machines.

If and When

~~~~~~~~~~~~~~~~~~~~~~

The nurse closed the door behind us. He checked to make sure my forms were in order, then sat me at a wooden school desk. I found myself wishing this test was like others I'd taken at a school desk, the questions a cause for anxiety but without significant bearing on my future. Alcohol was dabbed on my outstretched arm. I made a fist, gritted my teeth when the needle punctured my skin. As the hypodermic turned a dark garnet, I looked away, peering over the nurse's shoulder. Cardboard boxes were stacked at the far end of the room: disposable needles, cotton swabs, and rubber gloves. The world I knew had irreparably changed, and my history within it had been torn in two: before AIDS and after.

As my blood was drawn, I burned with one fierce and simple wish. I had wanted to love a man all my life, and now that I did, and he loved me back, I wanted us safe.

Two vials.

Three.

During the five years Brian and I had been living together, I heard about "gay cancer" with such terrible regularity that I'd grown wary of the phone, the radio, and the television, sure they would snag me in a web of bad news. Numbers rose. Risk factors were debated. The period of incubation extended further into the past. There seemed to be no way to absorb the damage or forgive the impotence of science, a Goliath felled by a virus. Keeping track of one's losses became a constant, morbid chore.

At the oddest moments — washing my car or paying a bill — I would suddenly realize that I no longer saw this or that man at the gym or the supermarket or walking his dog, and I would wish there was a way to find out what had happened to him. Should someone precede a sentence with "Remember so-and-so?" my heart would start pounding, and I felt almost gleeful if what followed was "He's being audited" or "He moved to Chicago." One day I saw the photograph of a man I'd slept with in the obituary of a local gay newspaper. I gripped the pages, tried to stretch the time since we'd been together — three years, four years, maybe five, long enough that I might be safe. When I ran into someone with whom I'd once had a sexual relationship, we'd greet each other with a sweet, disproportionate relief, as if we were long-lost kin. Beneath our greeting was a single unspoken exclamation: *You're still alive.*

I constantly feared for my own health, yet remained too afraid to get tested. In an effort to second-guess the odds, I tried to recall precisely what I had and had not done with each man I'd slept with before I'd met Brian, before I knew about the need to take precautions. Again and again, I replayed my sexual history, an urgent search for companionship after years of denying my desire for men. I remembered the scar on one man's stomach, the shifting muscle in another's back. If sex included penetration, I remembered who had entered whom. But there were still variables in the equation. Was oral sex a route of transmission? Was one exposure all it took? Had my partners been infected then? There were times I wished I could go back and undo every act that led to my present state of dread. But just as often, thinking of those nights with someone beside me, I felt vestiges of tenderness and pleasure that were stronger than any regret.

Brian was also reeling from the devastation of AIDS, but unlike me, he didn't torment himself by trying to predict the future of his health by examining his past. What's done is done, Brian said. Besides, there were so many unknowns. Practically every week doctors and scientists held a press conference in order to announce or retract yet another theory on the nature of the syndrome. There were cofactors to consider; excessive use of antibiotics and amyl nitrate were thought to be the most likely. Perhaps some men were born with a genetic constitution that made them either more susceptible or more resistant to infection. Shortly after a test for HIV antibodies was developed, Brian and I heard that the results were often inaccurate. One story blamed a false positive for the suicide of a young man in northern California. Health professionals were still debating the causal relationship between HIV and AIDS. Some said that a person might test positive for HIV but never develop any of the diseases associated with AIDS — unless, of course, the psychological blow of knowing you were positive weakened your immune system. According to the prevailing wisdom, it was irresponsible to get tested, and also irresponsible not to. Either choice exacted a price. For five years, Brian and I had been monogamous and practiced safe sex, and what we did now, he was quick to remind me, was the most we could hope to control. I couldn't imagine getting tested alone, so Brian promised he would take the test too, if and when I felt ready.

I might have held out even longer if my anxiety about AIDS hadn't turned me into a hypochondriac. Several times a day I felt my forehead, jumped on a scale, and pressed my glands. The absence of symptoms never quieted my fears but only convinced me that my symptoms were elusive. I scrutinized the lining of my eyes, the texture of my skin, and the forest of my scalp with an almost hallucinogenic intensity. After reaching a certain plateau of worry, I forgot what normalcy felt like, apart from the vague and nostalgic sense that I had once been a person who took his body for granted. Where I had once been drawn to the bathroom mirror in order to check the part in my hair or the fit of a shirt, I now stood before it endlessly, a man consulting an oracle, so close my breath would fog the glass. Every pore, every cell: unknowable and otherworldly. I stared and prodded. Talked myself into and out of panic. Fell down a narrow well of obsession.

One day I discovered a bump on my tongue that indicated, I was certain, the onset of AIDS. I began a relentless campaign to solicit medical opinions about the bump from my friends. That they knew no more about physiology than I did hardly mattered. Without giving it so much as a thought, I'd stick out my tongue in a restaurant, at a party, or after making a frantic dash across town to coax a diagnosis from someone new. "What is it?" I would ask, words garbled, tongue protruding. "Does it look dangerous? Should I go to the doctor? Is it . . . tongue-colored?" Ordinarily a patient man, Brian finally refused to look at my tongue one more time and suggested that I was experiencing a mild form of "conversion hysteria." In other words, emotional turmoil was taking a physical form. Although the vocabulary of Brian's profession has the power to summarize mental states, *conversion hysteria* was not a term I found very comforting. Whatever the psychotherapeutic name for it, all my thoughts and sensations seemed to converge on that tiny bump, as aggravating as a pebble in a shoe. Finally, my entire tongue began to ache, but it was impossible to tell whether this was an organic pain or the result of constantly twisting my tongue into odd angles so that it could be examined more closely. To my horror and fascination, the rearview mirror of my car slightly magnified the interior of my mouth. I knew things had gotten out of hand when I narrowly escaped a car crash while trying to get a better look.

"A dot?" asked the receptionist when I called the doctor for an appointment. I suddenly felt foolish for choosing that word. "On your tongue? And could you give me some idea of how big it is?" I was lost on a seesaw of relative sizes when she interrupted with, "Never mind, there's an opening tomorrow at two."

"I'm sorry," said Dr. Fernandez, rotating my head in the harsh light. "I don't see what you're talking about." He had no doubt been besieged by patients fearful of AIDS and assumed a sympathetic, if weary, tone. I pointed more fervently, my tongue going dry from exposure to air. "Tongues are like thumbprints," he said, tossing the wooden tongue depressor into the trash can and leaning against the sink. "The lumps and bumps, the topographical features, if you will, vary from person to person, and in some extreme cases —"

I told him not to go on. Dr. Fernandez asked me point-blank if I had been worried about AIDS. "If you find out you're positive, at least we can treat it early. There are more medications today than there were last month. Who knows what will happen somewhere down the road? The idea, my friend, is to stay alive as long as possible."

That, I agreed, was exactly the idea.

He rested his hand on my shoulder and urged me to take the test.

*

"Almost done," said the nurse as he extracted a final vial. This set of four samples made the test — Western blot — as statistically accurate as possible. The four vials were labeled with my identification number, then placed in an upright rack along with the blood of a dozen others who'd visited the clinic before me that morning.

Pressing a Band-Aid against the crook of my arm, I walked back into the waiting room, eager to find Brian. An entire wing of the Gay and Lesbian Community Services Center had been remodeled in order to accommodate the demand for testing. Muted colors, curved walls, and plush carpeting were meant to blunt one's apprehension. But the slick decor unnerved me, suggesting as it did that AIDS was here to stay, a plague so entrenched in daily life that buildings had time to rise around it. Soothing music wafted from built-in speakers, useless against the collective gloom. Several men and women were waiting their turn to take the test. A few people stared into space or at the flesh of their own hands. Some read the safer-sex brochure they'd been handed when they came in, though I suspected that many were thinking it was far too late to change the past, one instant of which might reverberate now, a dreadful echo.

I made my way toward Brian. He looked up from a magazine and suddenly paled with expectation, as if I might have the results right then. Just as we touched, the nurse called his number. I wished him luck, filled the warm impression he left in his chair, and watched him walk away. Thinning blond hair, square shoulders, tapered back — his body was a speech I could recite in my sleep.

As soon as he was gone, a video monitor in one corner began to play a series of interviews. People of various races, ages, and sexual orientations talked about the ways their lives had changed, and the ways they hadn't, after testing positive for HIV. Fear made it impossible for me to concentrate on what they were saying, but I appreciated the notes of hope that were strung like lanterns from voice to voice. I tried to listen. I shifted in my seat. I pressed the Band-Aid against my arm.

*

I'm not sure how Brian and I managed to stay sane for the two weeks before we could return to the clinic to learn the results. In retrospect, two weeks seems an unbearable wait. But we'd had two options, an "anonymous" or a "confidential" test, and we were afraid that even a confidential test with a private physician who would give us the results in two or three days might jeopardize our insurance. It was the late 1980s, a time when there were calls from politicians and religious leaders for quarantines and mandatory testing. One night on television, William F. Buckley, swiveling in his chair, calmly suggested tattooing the infected. The climate was one of vigilante logic, the proposals for what to do about AIDS as ravaging as the virus itself. An anonymous test had the least potential for repercussions, and a two-week wait was the price we had to pay.

Brian coped by working hard at the office. Listening to the problems of others offered him a respite from his own. After he came home, he'd change out of his dress clothes and busy himself in our yard, watering and potting plants, picking dead leaves from the annuals. It has always been his tendency to translate uncertainty into action, to combat fear with the ache of labor, and so he gardened even after dark. The odor of soil would seep into the house as though it were the scent of night itself. Looking up from a book, I'd remember the test with a start. Then I'd listen to the sounds of my lover's distraction, the brisk, continuous motion of a man awaiting his fate.

Every morning during the course of those two weeks, fear shook me awake like a chill. I was certain I would test positive. Too sleepy to govern my imagination, I pictured my face covered with lesions, my body gaunt and unfamiliar, a shunt plunging into my vein. With so many men falling ill around me, grim transformations were easy to imagine. But it was the unsharable nature of physical suffering that frightened me the most; like a thumbprint or a birthday, illness would belong to me alone, its privacy dividing me from Brian despite his powers of empathy and love.

Thirty-six years old, haunted by images of illness, I turned as wistful as an old man. Cells were fragile, skin porous, the bloodstream easily invaded. One night, while I lay on our bed lamenting the frailty of flesh, Brian walked in from the yard and undressed, his robust body a vivid contradiction.

Our erotic relationship had been a boon from the start, something about which I bragged to friends. We collided in bouts of breathless sex, and when it was over we fell away, sweating and incredulous, sometimes laughing at the sheer ferocity of our hunger for each other. So much of my life had been spent believing I might never touch a man that the sight of Brian naked beside me, beneath me, above me, has never lost its power to surprise. *At last*, a voice within me says, relieved by his proximity, grateful for his eagerness and heat.

During our two-week wait, I began to wonder whether I would allow myself to be touched with the same abandon if I knew I were infected and had, however remote, the potential to infect Brian. And what if my appearance (about which I have always been both vain and uncertain) were to change from the effects of illness? Who knew what reticence, what timidity, might paralyze me if I tested positive. Almost every night, with Brian sleeping quietly beside me, I imagined the end of our erotic life, my sadness so leaden and absolute, it took me a moment to realize that the results and all its ramifications were still days away.

Even when I was able to talk myself out of tragic plots involving my own health and its effect on my relationship with Brian, there was public hysteria to contend with. One afternoon I saw a TV preacher wailing about AIDS as God's retribution for immorality, and I spent the next two hours having heated, imaginary arguments with his hostile congregation. Another day I found myself frantically dialing a radio call-in show on which a city council person suggested that AIDS could be contracted from the drinking fountains in public buildings. I never got past a busy signal, and even if I had, I would have been apoplectic with anger. In fantasy, however, I was always more articulate and persuasive than I could ever be in real life, and my words caused all manner of ignorance and enmity to come to an end. Despite those impassioned, imaginary speeches, I was becoming more mistrustful of people than ever before, and I worried that my belief in people's decency and reason would become yet another loss to mourn. Though Brian held me when I felt overwhelmed, I told him only that I was afraid. There was no elaboration left to make. Fear was everywhere, hard and stark, and it rendered me speechless.

I rarely entertained the possibility that Brian might test positive. He seemed, if not unconcerned, less concerned than I, and coping with my own anxiety took most of my energy. Brian possesses an innate calm and, perhaps because of his profession, gives to his interactions with people a rare attentiveness. "We're going to be fine," he'd tell me. Certainty burned in his eyes, and I believed he was speaking from more than just a hunch. "You should start thinking," he said, "about what you're going to do with all your nervous energy after you test negative." Learning the results of my HIV test had become a dead end, a blind alley in time; I was glad to be asked to imagine an afterward. It was easy for me to lean on Brian, and he was soothed by soothing me. During those two weeks, he refused to become mired in worry. And as long as I could believe in Brian's luck, I could almost believe in my own.

*

Brian was not the kind of man I expected to end up with. I first saw him at Weight-Lifter's gym, shirtless and unself-conscious, easing his compact body through the room. He sang hello to friends, swung from the high bar, and paced in front of the mirror like a busy parrot. A bell and some seed, I thought to myself, and the picture would be complete. A brooder, a wallower in melancholy, I assumed my future lover would have to be a man as moody and interior as I. For the most part my friends were reticent and contemplative, artistic types whose most consistent trait was their unpredictability. A man with a direct and sunny disposition made me suspicious. I decided not to pay the talkative blond guy any attention; his looks probably got him enough.

In other words, I wanted him.

Brian swears that, after I finished working out that day, he followed me into the dressing room to get a better look. If he did, I don't remember. However nagging my loneliness, I was thick-headed when it came to flirtation, so uncertain about my effect on others that a guy practically had to whimper and scratch the ground before it occurred to me that he might be interested. I'd already convinced myself that Brian and I were incompatible and must have told myself, peeling off my damp sweatshirt while Brian hovered somewhere nearby, that his visit to the dressing room was merely a coincidence.

A few weeks later I saw Brian at the Detour, a crowded local bar. It took me a moment to recognize him through the cigarette smoke. He wore an old, olive drab Boy Scout shirt whose merit badges brought to mind every team and clique and fraternity to which I never belonged. The shirt was several sizes too small. Its snug fit gave the illusion that Brian had grown into a man that very evening and hadn't had time to change his clothes. There was something hormonal and endearing about the effect. I found myself walking toward him, electrified by my sudden nerve and the way Brian watched and welcomed my approach.

I'd be lying if I said our first conversation was anything but ordinary or claimed that we felt a strong intellectual connection. Haven't I seen you at the gym? Where do you live? What do you do? Brian told me he had moved to Los Angeles from Canada and had just started a private practice. I told him I taught English composition at a nearby college and was trying to write my first book. We exchanged halting sentences, shouted our vital statistics over the wail of Romeo Void. Soon the music grew so loud that the two of us were lip-reading, nodding and smiling at what we hoped were the appropriate parts, glad to have an excuse to concentrate on the mouth of the other. We were playing our roles in the theater of civilized mutual interest, all the while sniffing pheromones and guzzling beer and waiting to see which of us would muster the courage to ask the other home. At one point Brian excused himself. When he returned from the restroom, a couple of buttons had been undone and the shirt parted against his bare chest. I handed him a bottle of beer, a trophy for one of the most obvious attempts at seduction I had ever seen. He took a swig and his merit badges rippled. I liked where the night was leading; all along the way there loomed big, obvious billboards that read I WANT YOU and TAKE A GOOD LOOK. Our blunt interaction relieved me from guesswork and suggested that Brian was forthright and helpful. An ideal scout.

After our third beer, he asked me home. I ended up trailing his Toyota through the foothills. The lure of red taillights disappeared around the bends and reappeared on the straightaways. He hugged the curves, drawing me onward. Every now and then I could make out his silhouette as he lifted his head to catch sight of me in the rearview mirror. Satisfied that I was still behind him, he'd barrel ahead in a burst of speed. The hills were dark at that hour, the sky scoured by a Santa Ana. Stars glinted. Palm trees tossed. Long after we'd left the bar, the throb of music still boomed in my ears, a phantom soundtrack. I felt as if I were outside of myself, an audience of one, and I began to narrate the chase in the third person: *He steps on the accelerator and follows the hasty stranger up a gravel driveway.*

Once we'd parked our cars, Brian led me up a wooden staircase to his apartment, three small rooms above a garage. Standing behind him, I felt heat rise from the nape of his neck as he bent his head to find the right key. This glimpse of skin: that's all it took to make me hard. How had I been able to contain the need that was suddenly sweeping everywhere, as restless and charged as the air? I ran my hand down Brian's back, heard a click as the door unlocked.

As we stepped across the threshold, I held my breath and hoped there was nothing about his decor that would ruin the mood. Given my picky taste, that might have included any number of things: gold-veined mirrors, Parisian street scenes, crystal ashtrays, and any books or magazines that suggested a tendency toward sexism or an affinity for the Republican party. Imagine my joy when the door swung wide to reveal a kind of tree house, nothing in the living room except a futon, a pile of psychology books, and a view of the glittering, far-flung city.

A good man, an empty room. After a word or two about safe sex, we stripped off our clothes as if they'd caught fire, unfolded the futon, and tumbled onto it. Brian sometimes stopped in midkiss, slowly drew back, and held me by the shoulders. At arm's length, in the dim light, his throat and chest glistened where I'd licked them. Every time I glanced at his body I forgot myself entirely, desperate for the silken feel of his flesh. I felt like one of those game show contestants who's been put inside a glass booth and given only so many seconds to grab at a blizzard of one-dollar bills. The clock was ticking, there were countless sensations still left to try.

*

Over the next few months, our sex life thrived. But the longer our courtship continued, the clearer the differences in our taste and temperament became. Brian's apartment, and in some senses Brian himself, had been a kind of blank slate on which I secretly hoped to impose my aesthetic. I figured I would create an ally, a blond doppelganger with whom to share my interest in contemporary art and literature. There were trips to museums and a list of required reading in the guise of gift-wrapped books. Since I considered myself to be too psychologically sophisticated to try and mold another person, it never occurred to me that I was doing exactly that. Brian responded to Philip Glass and neoexpressionism with curiosity and intelligence, but in the end he was more taken with a Top 40 song or a platinum wig in a drag show.

I loved popular culture too, although in those days my identity was bound up in vanguard art — the more challenging, the better. Therefore it was hard to understand (some might say rationalize) many of the things that excited Brian. He was rapt, for example, when women were given makeovers on television. He'd hold his breath and wring his hands and shush me until the transformation was complete. Should the results displease him, he'd stomp his foot on the floor, and cry, "Her hair looks like a ratty bath mat!" If the woman's appearance had been improved, he'd whisper, "She's absolutely stunning." All right, I'd say to myself, think of these makeovers as the physical counterparts to the psychological transformations that are Brian's livelihood. Within minutes, however, all that powdering and tweezing would try my patience, and I'd find myself baffled by Brian's fascination.

If I wasn't convinced that Brian and I were meant to be a couple, neither was I convinced that we weren't. No sooner would I come to the conclusion that we were mismatched than I'd pine for his blue eyes, his tempered voice, his United Church of Canada calm. He possessed traits entirely different from those of my volatile, dark-haired Jewish relatives. Though Brian impressed most people as friendly and conventional, he seemed to me as exotic as a member of a lost tribe, his ritual handshakes and thank-yous an endless source of cross-cultural fascination. Every time I told myself I'd be better off with a grubby artist, I'd dream about his ribbed socks and the crackle of starch in his fresh white shirts.

Brian must also have questioned the wisdom of our relationship. In order to spend time with me, he suffered through mumbled poetry readings, senseless experimental films, and the disrobing of I don't know how many performance artists. He listened patiently when I questioned his reliance on statistics in order to understand patterns of human behavior. "What's meaningful is the exception," I'd argue, "not the rule." "But that's how I know the exception," he countered, "by understanding the rule." One Fourth of July night we smoked hashish and watched, from the windows of his apartment, fireworks pop and blossom above Dodger Stadium. "Oh my God," I said. "It's like a big advertisement for capitalism! Is there any phenomenon that isn't culture-bound? Has culture finally co-opted nature?" As I fretted and chewed my fingernails, Brian stared at the lights in the sky. "Oooh," he'd say, "that one was pretty."

These small conflicts and differences in perception made for some dicey, exciting times. The more dissimilar I thought we were, the more eager I was to establish contact, an astronomer waiting for radio signals from a distant world. But the greatest challenge was yet to come.

One year into our relationship, Brian considered buying a Cadillac. Not just any Cadillac, but a white Eldorado with gold trim. The advertisement claimed the car was "previously owned" rather than "used," a euphemism that embodied every ounce of snootiness I associated, fairly or unfairly, with the car itself. That my father had recently purchased the same make and model was reason enough, as far as I was concerned, for Brian not to buy it. Just seeing Brian behind the wheel would cast our relationship in an incestuous light, and though some men might be drawn to lovers who remind them of their fathers, I was not. I worried that his owning a Cadillac would affect me like aversion therapy, and I asked whether it was worth jeopardizing our extraordinary sex life for the kind of car driven by blue-haired matrons. In a last-ditch effort to change his mind, I listed aloud every negative association I had with Cadillacs: chandeliers, leisure suits, ostentatious watches, and Liberace.

Brian hooked his finger in my belt loop. "Come on," he said. "It's just a car."

His practice was picking up. He'd started to earn good money for the first time in his life. A double bed replaced the futon. He bought matching coffee mugs, new shirts for work. He was able to pay back his graduate school loans. How could I begrudge him the car he wanted? A friend of Brian's had convinced him that a "Caddy," as he put it, would be a good investment, so I blamed at least the initial idea on someone else. Besides, no matter what kind of car Brian drove, he would still be a patient, affectionate man, and his obstinance regarding the Caddy was attractive.

And so Brian traded in his innocuous old Toyota for a Cadillac Eldorado. I watched from his apartment window as he bobbed up the driveway, his face enveloped in a white, encroaching cloud. He appeared to have trouble with the power steering and wrestled with the wheel. The former owner's air freshener wagged back and forth from the rearview mirror. I put down my copy of *Remembrance of Things Past* and went to greet him. I could tell he was doubtful about his new purchase, though he grinned valiantly as he showed me the features. Air-conditioning. Cruise control. The dashboard boasted more buttons than the control room of a nuclear power plant. Windows, seats, doors, trunk: everything was automatic.

Brian treated me to a test drive. Normally as heedless as a cannonball, he now drove as timidly as the blue-haired matrons I'd warned him about. It wasn't his fault exactly; the sheer size of the car demanded that he proceed at a creep. The broad hood, viewed from within the passenger cabin, seemed to spill into the adjacent lanes. If a car passed in the opposite direction, we rocked in its wake, spared from impact by a couple of inches. No matter how cautiously a turn was executed, the car tilted at a drastic angle. This wouldn't have been so bad if the slick leather seats hadn't sent us sliding this way and that toward the shifting center of gravity. When I grabbed onto the padded door handle or placed my hand on the armrest for balance, they gave beneath my weight like sponge cake.

I turned toward Brian and tried to smile, but he was distracted by soft chimes and blinking lights; the car was making vain attempts to send a message. Brian flicked switches, poked at buttons. Later that night he was sure to lie awake with a full-blown case of buyer's remorse. I scolded myself for being so intolerant of his taste and reached out to squeeze his thigh.

Just as I vowed to give Brian a wider berth in our relationship, a car changed lanes in front of us. Through its rear window we could see a little girl playing with a Cabbage Patch Kid, a homely brand of doll that was all the rage among the prepubescent set. Its plump face bore two beady eyes, a pug nose, and a pouting mouth. Every doll was slightly different, the hair color and clothes giving it a unique identity and teaching children, I suppose, that each of us is special. I'd forgotten the travail of the Eldorado altogether and was thinking about the doll's cloying face and gingham dirndl, when I heard Brian ask me, "Aren't those dolls cute?"

A disagreement about a car or a painting or a piece of music was one thing, but, as much affection as I felt for Brian, it was inconceivable that I could devote myself to a man who thought a Cabbage Patch Kid was cute. A line had been crossed, the evidence against us too great to ignore. Though the car with the Cabbage Patch Kid turned the corner and disappeared, the damage, I feared, would last forever. My silence was conspicuous, especially in the airtight vacuum of the Cadillac.

"What's wrong?" asked Brian.

Earlier that week, I'd asked if he wanted to borrow *Remembrance of Things Past* after I was finished with it, and Brian had blithely said, "No thanks." He never could have guessed that, a few days later, his refusal would come back to haunt him.

"I would think," I said, raising myself in the white leather seat, "that you would find Marcel Proust every bit as interesting as a goddamn Cabbage Patch Kid!"

Too late, I was struck by the absurdity of my outburst. Why was I always prepared to discover an insurmountable difference, the rift that would finally divide us? Because I didn't want to lose him? There had been a note of the shrill English teacher in my voice, and I hated hearing it. I was trying to uphold my identity as an impassioned artist when the truth was I'd lost interest in Proust's story after his notorious bite of madeleine. I might not even finish the novel that, as I lay on my deathbed reviewing my life, would probably matter to me about as much as a Cabbage Patch Kid mattered to Brian.

"Look," said Brian, stepping on the gas. "I like what I like and you like what you like. Let's face it: we're a surprise to each other. That's the way it is and, if we stay together, that's the way it's going to be."

*

I let out a long, pent-up breath when told I'd tested negative, a man restored to the life he'd led, to the body in which his senses belonged. The counselor who sat before me, a tall woman with a boyish haircut, seemed fully aware of my relief and gratitude. She sat back and let me soak in my emotions, then asked if I'd spent much time considering the outcome of the test. At first I thought her question was rhetorical, a way of telling me she knew I'd been obsessed about AIDS. But she tilted her head and repeated the question. "Yes," I said. "I have spent a lot of time thinking about the test." The counselor asked if I was in a relationship, urged me to continue practicing safer sex with my partner, and held out a slip of paper with confirmation of my results. License, diploma, passport: to take it from her hands felt both auspicious and unreal. I remember thinking I could check the slip of paper in the middle of the night to make sure I'd heard her correctly. She opened the door to let me out, and whispered, "You're on your way."

Brian knew the results from the expression on my face. He reached up from his chair in the waiting room and grabbed my hand. He looked proud, as if I had accomplished something through hard work or an effort of will, where I saw myself as the random, giddy recipient of grace. When the counselor called out Brian's number, I let go of his hand and dropped into a chair.

It had been nearly six years since we'd met. The Cadillac had come and gone. We shared a house, meals, chores. The night before, like every night since we'd lived together, we reached for each other's bodies in our sleep and found a groggy solace. That morning we awoke earlier than usual, allies who ate and dressed in silence, about to find out how the future would unfold.

I postponed my own relief while Brian met with the counselor; wishing him well was an all-consuming labor, as if I were sculpting, from a block of marble, the moment he'd return with good news. Since we'd walked into the clinic, I'd been afraid to jinx the future by hoping too hard for something good. If Brian tested negative, the future would be receptive to projections, and for the first time in quite a while, I wasn't too superstitious to imagine us growing old together, turning the grindstone of minor disagreements, having marathons of risky sex.

Dazed as I might have been while inside the consultation room, some part of me had measured and memorized the exact length of time it took to be informed that I was healthy. Those two minutes passed. No sight of Brian. I must have said "Oh no" out loud, because a couple of people in the waiting room glanced in my direction. My muscles tightened, jaw clenched, body braced against the blow I feared most. Brian finally opened the door and signaled me inside.

*

On our way back to the car, Brian told me I was free to leave him if I felt I couldn't face what was to come. The proposition was unthinkable, and I told him so, but I was also seized by an impulse to flee from the sharp, intractable facts. I walked without the sensation of moving, touched Brian without the satisfaction of making contact. Arrival and rest were impossible concepts, and for a moment I felt certain we would never be able to find the car or our way back home. We walked down a side street, weeds stitching the broken pavement. Because anything I might say or do, short of saving him, would make no difference, a future of speech and action seemed pointless. Still, I took his keys, told him I would drive, and stamped our despair with the repeated assurance that I loved and would stay beside him no matter what. To add "no matter what" swung the future wide open to anguish, and I wished I hadn't said it. Brian sat in the passenger seat. He looked out the window and then down at himself with numb surprise, as if his body were another object in the distance. "I feel fine," he kept protesting. Caught in traffic, it occurred to me that we hadn't cried; there had been only our fast, defeated breathing as we tried to listen to the counselor, whose every consolation I'd instantly forgotten.

"Better it's me," said Brian. "You're so afraid of illness."

"I don't care what it takes. . . ." I said, but didn't know how to finish the sentence. The second I gave myself over to hope, hope was diluted with pessimism, then pessimism infused with hope. Brian would survive. Brian would die. Possibility chased its tail. And so it would go for the rest of the day, for weeks on end, for years to come: I rally and cower, rally and cower, and no matter how well we adapt to his "status," no matter how nobly he rolls with the blows, I'm lessened by the virus that, day by day, dominates my lover's blood.

As I drove us home that morning, I felt myself graze, again and again, the rough edge of anger, though I wasn't sure toward whom or what. *Time* magazine had recently shown a photograph of the HTLV III virus on its cover, and it seemed absurd to direct my rage toward a tiny, mindless particle. NIH, CDC, HHS — all the bureaucratic acronyms came to mind, as senseless as words in a foreign language. In all likelihood Brian had contracted AIDS from his former lover, Vinnie, who had tested positive the year before. But there was no way to be sure, and I didn't have the stomach to blame a man who, in the photographs Brian had of him, wore thermal underwear and a red fez; as far as I was concerned, Vinnie's lavish mugging was proof of his innocence, and the innocence of thousands like him.

As we turned onto our street, the neighborhood's familiar, sheltering trees made more acute the notion that everything had changed. I was not a person who prayed, and the greater my need to bargain with God, the more I felt estranged from him, or at least from the God whose followers despised me, who would think AIDS a fitting punishment for daring to touch another man.

Brian and I had taken the day off from work, and as soon as we unlocked the front door, he went to tend the garden and I went to wash the dishes. We assumed these small tasks without saying a word, clinging to our chores as though they might protect us, might press us snugly back into our lives. I rolled up my sleeves, stoppered the sink. It struck me that the house was teeming with bacteria, a whole new species of adversary, and I let the faucet run until it scalded. No measure of cleanliness, however, could spare Brian from infection once his body grew indiscriminate and thin, ready to admit the world. Steam beaded the kitchen window.

Dishes from our breakfast lay beneath the water, as ancient and dim as a shipwreck.

Years' worth of small assertions — holding hands in public, introducing ourselves as a couple to a new neighbor — had gone into the simple thing we'd become: men who shared the same bed. And now our life together was at stake. "It's come to this," I said to myself. Just as this surge of self-pity threatened to overwhelm me, Brian walked inside bearing a fistful of irises. He lay them on the cutting board, sliced their stems, and arranged them in a vase. When he set them on the kitchen counter, we stared at their spotted yellow throats. Soon I sensed that Brian's silence had turned pensive, and I asked him what he was thinking, certain he'd answer "AIDS."

"I'm wondering," he said, "what should I plant in the flower bed next year?"

At that point, neither of us knew the condition of his immune system, his T-cell count or antigen level. Trouble might be years away or close at hand; the perpetual tests, the nervous mathematics, were yet to come. If, by planning ahead, Brian was avoiding the gravity of his circumstance, the limitations of time, who could blame him. Optimism was precisely the point of view that would sustain him, would make his sero-status easier for both of us to bear. Too frequently, I'd heard the word *denial* used to describe anyone who wasn't chained to misfortune like a dog to a post. In all probability Brian would live to see another year, and believing in its advent, denying that it might be otherwise, flooded the room like a sweet anesthetic. I grasped his shoulders and turned him toward me. "I know this is really corny," I said, "but my life would be nothing without you."

Brian laughed. "I feel exactly the same way," he said. "My life would be nothing without me."

*

We did everything in our power to slip through the rest of that day as though it were like any other. And yet, no matter how artful our pretense, ordinary acts sagged under the pressure of our new knowledge. We ate lunch, watched the news, and walked the dog, our routines colored by — or rather drained of color by — the fact that they were finite. Of course I always knew that Brian would die one day, as would I, but it seemed as if we had, up until now, escaped our debt to mortality, had somehow delayed it or held it in abeyance with the sheer, unwitting strength of our contentment. I worried that his death, like oxygen or time, would become the medium in which we'd live.

I embraced Brian as often as possible, but it was as if we were composed of different electrical charges or chemical compounds, and I thought about our sero-status every time we touched. Though I would later learn to accept our separateness with greater equanimity, and even to be glad I'd tested negative, that day I refused to submit to our difference, and tried to bridge the gulf between us with physical affection. Reaching out to him felt unfamiliar; I found myself gauging each embrace: too protective and it might suggest he couldn't take care of himself, too blasé and it wouldn't fairly represent the depth of my concern, too desperate and it might suggest that I crumpled at the first sign of crisis, a mate who wouldn't be sturdy if and when Brian grew weak. Yet Brian leaned against my chest, too tired to notice my busy implications. The heat of his skin, the density of his flesh, saddened as soon as it soothed me. His body was the very balm I needed because his body was what I stood to lose.

I spent the late afternoon phoning the handful of friends who knew we were expecting our test results. It seemed best to side-step formalities and simply blurt the bad news. If my friends were hopeful, I turned grave, and if they turned grave, I bolstered their hope. In either case, I wasn't sure which I felt myself. I watched Brian through the window as I talked. He staked wisteria vines to a trellis and watered pots of salvia. The dog curled near him, uncomprehending. Both of them lost definition in the dusk. As darkness fell, I wanted the sky to tighten like a lid, sealing off that day forever.

Everything we had been doing sexually for the last six years had proven safe; I'd learned as much that very morning. And yet, as I slid into bed with him that night, dread outweighed my better judgment, went against everything I knew to be true about the transmission of AIDS. We kissed and his mouth felt alien, wet and deep with potential harm. What if he had somehow punctured his gums and I had bitten my lip? What if I licked his throat where he'd nicked himself with the razor? What if our blood were mingling at that very moment, this kiss the pivot on which my future turned?

What if, what if. No matter how fiercely I pressed against him, the sound of uncertainty couldn't be muffled. I envisioned our bodies riddled with fissures, microscopic points of entry, our skin a weave as loose as gauze. I lay there reciting statistics to myself: *No cases of AIDS have been linked to kissing. Oral sex is safe before ejaculation.* What I wouldn't have given to hear, instead of my failed attempts at reason, the clamor of want.

I swept my hands down Brian's stomach, along the inside of his thighs. He returned my half-hearted kisses, his touch aggressive and reticent by turns. Neither of us, I think, had ever felt the need to achieve anything, apart from the pyrotechnics of pleasure, by making love. And now we expected the act of sex to erase our trepidation, to prove that our physical history would not be changed by AIDS. The burden made us soft. Turned us into strangers.

*

Brian continued to see clients from early in the morning till late into the night. As always, in the unscheduled time between sessions, he typed his notes, balanced accounts, stocked up on Kleenex and instant coffee. While waiting for the results of his first T-cell test, he was spared from constant worry by his obligation to clients. Only when he came home, he told me, did anxiety begin to sink in. Something about the quiet house, the dark rooms beyond his reach, the dog watching his every move. Since I took it upon myself to clean the house and wash the clothes, there was nothing Brian had to do once he walked through the door except unknot his tie, step out of his shoes, put his clients' problems behind him, and listen to the hum of his own emotions. "What we're waiting for," he reminded me one night, "is just numbers on a piece of paper. How I feel is more important, and as of now I'm feeling fine." Yet both of us knew we would read those numbers as if they were leaves at the bottom of a teacup.

If Brian indulged his anxiety mostly at night, my schedule of reckoning was entirely different. Even before I opened my eyes, before the room took shape around me, before I felt the weight of the blanket, the heat of his body next to mine, I sensed a threat to Brian's life. Apprehension came with my waking, a stone lodged in consciousness, hardened by the depth and pressure of sleep.

Unable to write, teaching only two nights a week, I had the whole day to entertain catastrophe. I fortified myself with worry, imagining the worst so that if the worst should come to pass, it wouldn't be unexpected as well as awful. My fantasies of abandonment were so thorough — Brian's T cells dwindle, the treatments fail, his suffering is over, my loneliness begins — that when he came home I was startled to see him, as though he'd come back from the afterlife instead of a day at work.

As it turned out, Brian's T cells were in the 1100s, high even for an HIV-negative person, who has an average of 800 to 1200. The percentage of helper to suppressor cells also fell within the normal range. We were elated, though the doctor explained that there was always the possibility of a statistical fluke, some error at the laboratory that could skew the results. After all, Brian had been infected at least six years ago, and the doctor thought the test would have registered a few changes, however slight, in his immunity. He suggested that Brian retake the T-cell test.

Brian had called me from his office to tell me the news.

"What do you think?" I asked him.

"I have no idea what to think. The next test will tell."

And so began a lifetime of tests, and our avocation of waiting.

No sooner had I hung up the phone than I found myself wanting to believe that Brian's HIV test, not his T-cell count, would prove to be the error. As a child, bored with the laws of probability, with the stale physics of the everyday, I held my breath, focused my eyes, and tried to move an inanimate object — a pencil or a paper clip — with a blast of sheer concentration. Though the object before me never budged, I swore I saw it shift position. And there I was, thirty years later, funneling my concentration, pitting my wishes against the facts.

*

The next T-cell test wasn't quite so encouraging. And three months later, the numbers and percentages dropped to about six hundred. Friends who had undergone years of T-cell tests assured Brian he would get used to taking them. "It's all relative," insisted one friend with four hundred or so T cells. "You feel sorry for yourself until you hear about someone whose numbers are even lower than your own. Eventually you just pay attention to the general direction: up or down. Then even up or down hardly matters, as long as they don't go down by much." A friend of a friend felt he had improved his count with acupuncture and a macrobiotic diet, while another credited lots of fun and frozen dinners. A friend of a friend of a friend, a skier with only two T cells left, had just returned from Arrowhead, and though we'd never met the man, we were unreasonably happy to hear about his ski trip.

Like campers huddled around a fire, we were mesmerized by T-cell lore. The moral of every story seemed to be the same: one had to unhitch himself from statistics, had to be greater than the sum of his cells. The protagonists of some tales were healthy while others were ill, but each had found a way to face the future, either by surrendering to, or raging against, uncertainty.

For every story of endurance, there was an equal and opposite story of degradation. A former client of Brian's approached us at a restaurant one night and sat heavily in a vacant chair. Having no idea that Brian was positive, he told us how he came home one day to discover his lover, who had twenty T cells and suffered from dementia, trying to eat the kitchen sponge. "When I went to take the sponge away, he bawled like a kid and asked me what was happening." A lanky man in his mid-twenties, he closed his eyes as he spoke, laboring to reconstruct the scene, as if it had happened long ago to some other unfortunate couple. "I can't stand to see him this way," he continued. "And I can't stand to leave him alone. I'm afraid he's going to get lost in our house. Christ, he might as well have Alzheimer's. Sometimes I feel like we're a hundred years old." Brian put down his fork. He responded softly, offering suggestions. But I wondered if Brian pictured himself, if only for a vivid instant, unable to recognize food.

Anything could happen. Any disease, or set of diseases, might lurk around the corner. Bacterial, mental, neurological. Meningitis, toxoplasmosis, cytomegalovirus. From a vista of possibilities, those affected with HIV, and those in love with those affected, can pick an enormous number of fates, trying each one on for size. Even back then, I had an inkling that once Brian actually suffered from an HIV-related illness, once he confronted something concrete, the scope of fate would begin to narrow;

the illness at hand would have a name, would require a specific course of action. Until then the future was incalculably grim.

I don't know how I would have survived those first few months if our almost constant anxiety hadn't been leavened by Brian's humor. Morbid jokes and sarcastic asides erupted from him without warning. One Sunday, for example, I saw him reading obituaries in the newspaper, a weekly ritual that a positive test did nothing to curtail. Several of Brian's clients were people with AIDS; he counseled the families of terminally ill men; he lectured on safer sex for a group called the Life Savers; he spoke at the funerals of his teachers and colleagues. Facing death had become an everyday occurrence and, like a priest or a surgeon, he developed the detachment necessary to perform his job. This detachment allowed him to read the obituaries without the dread one might expect, yet his reading them surprised me. "Don't the obituaries depress you?" I finally asked him. "How can you read them?"

Brian slowly put down the paper, his movements unnaturally stiff and mechanical, his eyes wide. "Because," he droned, mimicking an android, "I do not possess your bothersome and petty human emotions."

I often found myself laughing hysterically and unpredictably in those days, like someone bursting through the surface of water and gulping air. One joke in particular struck me as the funniest thing I'd ever heard. It went something like this:

Three explorers are hacking their way through a tropical jungle when they are captured by a band of primitive tribesmen. Back at the village, the tribesmen tie the explorers to stakes and the villagers gather around. The chieftain of the tribe walks up to the first explorer, and says, "You must make your choice. Death, or Umbabwah."

Hmm, thinks the first explorer. I guess anything is better

than death. "All right," he says to the chieftain, "I choose Umbabwah."

With that, the first explorer is untied and the villagers drag him into the bushes where the men and women pile on top of him, fucking and sucking in a wild orgy that lasts for hours.

After they are spent, the chieftain walks up to the second explorer, and says, "You must make your choice. Death, or Umbabwah."

That wasn't so bad, thinks the second explorer. "All right," he says to the chieftain. "I choose Umbabwah, too."

The second explorer is untied and dragged into the bushes where there's moaning and groaning, and every imaginable kind of sex takes place in every position for several more hours.

Finally, the chieftain approaches the third explorer and says, "You must make your choice. Death, or Umbabwah."

"That is the most disgusting show of pagan depravity I have ever seen," cries the third explorer. "I will choose death!"

"Very well," says the chieftain. "Death it shall be. But first, a little Umbabwah."

I told that joke repeatedly and took it personally when people didn't laugh at the punch line. It *was* personal. Though I couldn't have put it into words at the time, that joke embodied my own dilemma: reconciling my desire for Brian and my fear of infection. In the jungle of that joke, each explorer must give in to primitive, libidinal impulses. Making a choice between sex and death is a mere illusion; both, as the chieftain knew all along, are inevitable.

*

AIDS turned desire into challenge, a dare. Desire was the haven at the center of a maze, and I had to wend my way down misleading paths and to plenty of dead-ends in order to return there.

Along the way, there sometimes seemed to be no boundary between public and private fear; reading an interview with someone who insisted he'd contracted AIDS through a mosquito bite, or hearing about someone who sued an HIV-positive doctor for failing to disclose his sero-status, would leave me uncertain and churning for hours. If everyone else was this afraid of AIDS, maybe I should be terrified, too. AIDS might be more contagious than I thought. What I knew to be proven fact and what I worried might be true wrestled together like hulking bears. The only advantage to these psychological grudge-matches was that they left me so drained I finally gave in to a kind of exhausted abandon. Fine, I would think, drinking Brian's kiss when he walked through the door, if this is lethal, it's how I want to go.

For a while, any obvious attempts at safer sex — trying fellatio with condoms, for example, with its fumblings and apologies and nervous laughter, reminded us we were a sero-different couple. Donning that condom was a little like wearing an asbestos suit and trying to forget you're walking through fire. Our self-consciousness became a third party who crawled into bed with us, cajoling and cheering and shouting directions; however well intended, its presence between the sheets was distracting.

It took several months after we'd taken our HIV tests for our sex life to return to normal. I realize that many people entertain grave doubts as to the normalcy of same-sex relationships in the first place, and in some sense, it was precisely my internal arguments with such people that helped restore my sex life with Brian. *How can you two still have sex?* an imagined skeptic would ask me. *How can you play Russian roulette with your life now that you know your partner is positive?* He's been positive all along, I'd remind them, and I've stayed negative. Slowly, deliberately, I'd explain to them the rules of safer sex, citing statistics and going so far as to list a few of the specialties on the menu — frottage, massage, mutual masturbation — that don't put one at risk. By convincing them I knew what I was doing, I gathered the broken bits of my conviction. Wouldn't the skeptics be asking the very same questions about our physical involvement if AIDS didn't exist? *How can you have sex with a man? You're ruining your life!* Listen, I'd say when no other argument worked, I'd rather be dead than alive and afraid of having sex with my lover.

Refusing to treat Brian like a pariah set me apart from the guests on talk shows who announced, with what I couldn't help but see as a kind of fearful zeal, that celibacy was the only answer. In the face of AIDS, they sternly advised, run the other way. In an attempt to single-handedly dam the tide of human sexual response, some of them suggested AIDS was proof that sex outside of marriage is wrong. But if married couples also got AIDS, weren't they saying that sex itself is wrong? The more I heard about the infamy of sex, the more determined I was to have it, to cultivate my craving for Brian.

That I found him beautiful made this easier. Once the shock of his positive test began to fade, I could see him as he hoped to see himself: the same man as before, infected with a virus. I'd watch him emerge from the shower; wiping the misted mirror, he'd appraise his wet reflection. More persuasive than debates with imaginary foes, stronger than my fear of infection, there existed the pull of my lover's body, irresistible, definitive.

Disease might make him a ragged, abject man, but every fear about what might befall him was countered by the memory of sex: the heat of his thighs as he straddled my stomach, sweat beading on his shoulders and chest. When I asked myself, as Brian had once asked me, if I'd rather be free of our relationship, I'd think about drawing him down to the bed, and the answer no would always come back with the same unvarying odds as an echo.

Brian felt the burden of responsibility when it came to making love. "I'd die if you got it," he once confessed. But the less I worried, the more he relaxed, and the more he relaxed, the less I worried. The knot of inhibition loosened. We enjoyed testing our return to sex, scientists who performed the same experiment again and again just to rejoice in the unchanging outcome. Raising an eyebrow or staring at each other an instant too long became a signal to rush into the bedroom. To try another impromptu reunion. To see if we could hold onto caution and throw it to the wind.

If I thought about AIDS while we made love, for the most part those thoughts were fleeting, as remote and muffled as sounds from the street. Sex became an empirical matter: I concentrated on the things I could see — Brian's ribs, the small of his back, the arch of his ass as he lay on his stomach — instead of on the things I couldn't — platelets, bacteria, virus. While our hearts were racing, skin hot to the touch, the visible world of weight and shape took precedence over the realm of minutiae. For a few blessed seconds we tensed in release, hurling away from worry.

In the aftermath I sometimes went into the bathroom and rinsed with mouthwash or took a shower, refusing to scold myself or wonder if Brian might be insulted. Hundreds of other couples, positive or not, did the same after sex. A few precautionary rituals, necessary or not, were preferable to the hypochondria that had once overwhelmed me, and in the end they seemed no more unusual than loosening my belt after a good meal.

Padding back into the bedroom, I'd find Brian petting Zack, who'd leapt on the bed for scraps of affection. "We love you, too," Brian would assure him. "But in a different way." The dog crooned and twisted in the blanket, nose pressed against the embers of our scent.

*

First came small, chronic problems. Persistent athlete's foot that over-the-counter sprays and tinctures held in check. For the canker sores that lingered and stung more than usual, Brian was prescribed Zovirax Suspension, a numbing cherry swig of which he held in his mouth for a full minute, then swallowed in a single gulp. After he developed a sensitivity to fleabites, we exiled the dog from our bed and, three or four times a year, sprinkled the house with an organic flea repellent that had to be left on the floor for twenty-four hours, a kind of gritty, unseasonable snow. Fermented food made Brian's eyes water and his nose run, so he avoided soy sauce, yeast, and alcohol. Week by week, month by month, the list of proscriptions grew longer.

When his T cells consistently numbered under five hundred — three consecutive tests with similar results constituted an upward or downward "trend" — he began, after much deliberation, a regimen of AZT. It was around this time that other antiviral medications (ddI and ddC) were approved for widespread use; these drugs could be taken in different combinations with AZT, and it was hoped that one's immune system might never grow inured to their effect. We put our faith in permutations and were granted, for a while at least, the luxury of believing that everyone infected with HIV might one day thrive, or at least buy time, on an ever expanding cycle of drugs. The most optimistic among the medical community compared HIV to diabetes, a chronic disease that pharmaceuticals might arrest like a freeze-frame explosion.

The jargon of science became a kind of anthem, proof of our commitment to negotiate with the disease by speaking its language. When keeping friends abreast of Brian's condition, I heard myself speaking in tongues: "The doctor is considering a prophylaxis of aerosol pentamadine if the next test shows a decline in the ratio of helper to suppressor cells." The syllables felt good in my mouth. Having mastered the words, I'd also mastered, or so it seemed as long as I kept talking, the disease to which the words referred.

In truth, I often felt confused by medical terminology, cursing myself for faking my way through biology in high school, an even rudimentary understanding of which might help me now. The more knowledge I tried to amass, the further behind I seemed to fall. I subscribed to a newsletter that featured articles, in both Spanish and English, about dozens of new drug trials, therapies, and nutritional supplements: "AZT-Resistant Strains of HIV"; "ddI Safety Summary"; "Kaposi's Update"; "Overview of Antiretroviral Therapy"; "Kombucha Mushroom, Hope or Hype?" But after reading a few pages, the boldfaced headlines, the raw data, the graphs and statistics, blurred together. There were times I had to bow out and let Brian cope with the glut of information on his own. I wanted to apply my knowledge like a poultice, but the virus thrived in Brian's blood, and no degree of expertise could change the fact that we lived in different bodies.

As quickly as HIV could stir my sense of attachment, it could accentuate our separateness. When I saw his arm or buttocks bruised by a needle, simple words like "us" and "we" suddenly lost their power. Still, Brian used those words as often as I did: "We'll see what the doctor says when he calls us." Though he never expected me to share the responsibilities of his illness beyond, say, asking me to remind him to take his pills after dinner, we talked about his health as often as we discussed finances or errands. While those discussions felt alien to the life we had known before HIV, that life also felt alien, a dimly remembered dream. If I could say little else good about living with someone positive, I could at least say this: to know, at any given moment, the chemistry of Brian's blood, his T-cell count and liver function, the ecology of his skin and mouth and bowels, made our intimacy as rich and carnal as any I'd ever known.

With his itinerary of tests and doctor's appointments, Brian also became versed in the magical chants, the chilly lyricism, of medical terms. *Peptides, nucleosides, reverse transcriptase.* Having studied physiology and chemistry in college gave him a head start in the scholarship of his own survival. How many men and women, I wondered, had become more fluent in that tricky Latinate vocabulary than they ever thought possible. And how many others had thrown up their arms, the mutiny of their cells too complex to comprehend.

Daily doses of AZT reminded Brian of his HIV status and made him think of himself as sickly despite his energy and sense of well-being. Yet he experienced no adverse side effects and felt safer taking it than not. In an effort to make his treatment as comprehensive as possible, he supplemented doses of AZT with herbs prescribed by a holistic doctor who visited America every few months from England. After their consultations, Brian carried away brown paper bags filled with pungent roots, dried buds, and crushed leaves, substances whose exotic names and curative effects he had all but forgotten by the time he got home. We sat down in front of the television and, while governments toppled, stocks rose and fell, and celebrities denied the latest scandal, dragged hundreds of clear gel capsules through the mounds of herbs we'd poured onto dinner plates. Pressing the fragile halves together, the two of us averaged about eight capsules per minute. The work was as slow and exacting as needlepoint. By the time we were through our fingers ached, and the air was thick with herbal dust.

This East-West cocktail of herbs and AZT seemed to do the trick. Nearly a year went by relatively free of illness and incident. Then an outbreak of small clear bumps appeared near Brian's temples. The dermatologist diagnosed molluscum, a skin condition common among people with HIV, and prescribed an ointment of glycolic acid. Concerned about his appearance, Brian covered the most noticeable spots with make-up before we went out. Molluscum was the first overt symptom, and its visibility required yet another adjustment; soon his body would show the signs, and not just to us but to the world at large. Once the molluscum on his face was somewhat under control, it spread to the inside of his thighs. These the doctor froze with liquid nitrogen. The scabs took weeks to heal, and I was careful not to touch or put any pressure on them during sex. The sight of them made me squeamish, caused distracting pangs of sympathy, and I worried Brian might see me looking and become self-conscious. Avoiding the inside of his thighs seemed a small sacrifice for the warmth and pleasure of physical contact, but I realized that the two of us would have to make an ever-increasing set of concessions if we were to keep our erotic life intact.

Late at night, unable to sleep, I'd wonder how many changes Brian's body would have to undergo before it looked entirely different from that of the man I'd met long ago. How many blows can desire bear, how many challenges, modifications? As I tossed and turned, the diminishments of HIV would appear to me as the hallway in a fun house I'd visited as a child; the corridor grew more and more narrow till I had to turn sideways, then suck in my stomach and hardly breathe, then walk in careful, crablike steps to squeeze through the exit. Except, in this case, there was no exit.

In the mornings after those restless nights, I'd grab Brian the second he stirred, excited by his skin as I reached beneath his T-shirt. If his thighs were sore, his stomach was not; if his hands were numb from neuropathy, his armpits and chest were sensitive; if canker sores meant we couldn't deep-kiss, the surface of his lips assumed a warm importance. For every sense that had been denied us, another sense grew more acute. We were like blind men who, undaunted by darkness, find their way by sound and touch.

*

That summer I volunteered at the Necessities of Life program in Los Angeles, an organization that provides groceries to people with AIDS. My job was simple: after taking an order form from another volunteer, I filled a large shopping cart with a more or less uniform supply of staples: bread, rice, beans, canned and fresh vegetables, toilet paper, soap, and disposable razors. These I gathered from bins and metal shelves that ran the length of a warehouse. I double-checked the order once the cart was full, then wheeled it to the "client" who sat in a makeshift waiting room talking to other clients or reading one of the donated copies of *Life*, *People*, or *Vanity Fair*. Again and again, I'd emerge from the aisles to discover that the client was someone I recognized from the days when I was single, one of the hundreds of faces I'd glimpsed on the street, in restaurants or bars. Some of these men had grown gaunt and puzzled since I'd last seen them, while others were as fit and alert as ever. In any case, they all had AIDS. And here we were in an echoing warehouse, nodding as we might have years ago. After the jolt of recognition, there was nothing much to do except bag their groceries, and nothing much to say except, "I've seen you before," "Can I help you with these?" "Take care of yourself," and "Good-bye."

By summer's end, I braced myself every time I wheeled a cart toward a client, wondering if I'd find yet another acquaintance waiting for his weekly ration of food. A generation of men were dying, dead. Without the backdrop of familiar peers, my past grew harder to recognize.

Then there were the friends for whom one has to reserve the full strength of one's grief and frustration and disbelief. Jim and Ken and Terry and Bill. I tried not to extrapolate from every tragedy and apply it to Brian. But certain deaths were especially foreboding, and the connection to Brian waited to be made.

Eventually, I joined a drop-in group for the HIV-negative partners of men who were positive. This was the first time I'd ever taken advantage of a community mental health service, and in order to do so I had to rid myself of an aversion to group therapy, which I pictured as a bedlam of weeping and shouting and group hugs.

In fact, our meetings were fairly subdued, colored in large part by the shock and melancholy you might expect from people who've been forced to yield their lovers to a virus. About ten of us showed up for each meeting. Our partners were in different stages of the disease, from asymptomatic to one man who, wasting away despite infusions of Pamalar, had just been admitted to the intensive care unit at the hospital where we met. Led by a facilitator whose partner was positive, we sat in a circle and took turns talking. At times our discussions were strictly pragmatic: when to begin a prophylaxis for MAI, what brands of bottled water are least likely to carry microbes, how someone's lover could apply for disability without having to wade through a swamp of paperwork. Other topics were less easily resolved. At almost every meeting, one man among us was desperate and obsessing about an ailment that plagued his lover and whose source or treatment could not be found. We'd hear him out, then admonish him to focus on his own well-being; what good would it do if he didn't eat or sleep himself? But each of us understood the temptation to lose ourselves in our partner's illness, to try and save his life with a dose of pure concern. Since we tended to vacillate between two moods — grinding worry and tense determination — peace of mind boiled down to this: one had to let go of both hopelessness and hope, a trick we might manage for seconds at a stretch.

Newcomers always wanted to know right off the bat whether any of us still had sex with our partners. Each of us would tell him when we last made love, what we would and wouldn't do in bed. M. wasn't comfortable getting fucked by his lover even with a condom, while J. was a fearless French-kisser, though it was all a moot point to L., whose lover had shingles and couldn't lie on his back let alone make love. Airing our sex lives came to seem no more embarrassing than divulging our shoe size.

A few who visited the group were young enough to have little or no recollection of life before AIDS, and one night a young man asked the rest of us, hardly senior citizens ourselves, to tell him what that life had been like. He leaned forward, propped his chin on his fist. How could we describe those days of abandon? Bodies ended their solitude by burrowing into other bodies. And the consequence of such recklessness? Flesh-wrenching pleasure. I wanted to tell the boy something I couldn't articulate at the time: before AIDS, sex and death were like figures on opposite sides of a coin; they gazed in different directions, not into each other's eyes. "It was really different," was all I could say. "Satisfaction on tap," another man added. "The most you risked was a broken heart." Nodding at everything we said, the boy had no idea which of our statements were accurate and which were lit by the glow of nostalgia. We might as well have been describing Shangri-la, so far-fetched was sex without fear.

Many nights a theme emerged. Religion, for instance. F. told us a Baptist minister arrived unannounced at his apartment door one morning. The minister had been sent by his lover's mother to try to convert her son, who could barely sit up. F. didn't want to let the minister in, but his lover, high on morphine-drip, moaned from the bedroom that he didn't mind, he was bored to death, even a Baptist didn't sound so bad, and it might keep his mother quiet for a while. "Better get right with God before the Rapture," warned the minister, hovering beside the bed. F. stood close and folded his arms. He swore he saw his lover's expression, bemused at first, give way to doubt. A Baptist in their bedroom was cruel and intrusive, like a virus invading the blood. "If you want to do something to help him," he imagined telling the minister, "if you have half the compassion you claim, then get into bed with him every night like I do." After the minister had said his piece, F. led him to the door and slammed it. Not only was he mad at the minister, he resented his lover for listening, for having a mother, for lying in bed.

G. said most of his Jewish relatives try their best to accept his seven-year relationship with a man who has AIDS. Only one aunt, for all her good intentions, makes hurtful remarks. "You're lucky to be negative," she tells him. "My lover is dying," he snapped back, "and you're telling me I'm lucky? Might as well say Anne Frank was lucky in her attic: cozy and quiet, no phones or distractions, food brought to the door."

Hardest for me were the nights when someone would imagine life without his lover. The bed is empty, the days too long. No one will ever love him so much. Laundry and bills and dust pile up. Families argue, friends defect. An endless list of deprivations, some of them reasoned, others absurd. One by one the rest of us chimed in, a mournful chorus. I balked at the thought, and my preface never varied: "If and when Brian dies . . ." *If and when.* I say it to this day. I edge toward the inevitable, bring myself to the precipice, and will not look down. I hold out, hold on, with this one refusal.

It would be too simple to say that I gleaned a lesson from each of the men in that group. Their stories did not instruct like fables, could not be wrung or rendered for comfort. More often than not, the stories told in that room frightened me with their uncertainty, bitterness, and turns for the worst. Yet whenever I listened to someone else, I heard in that person my surfeit of feeling. And when it came my turn to speak, I welcomed a brief, tenuous relief as my life with Brian rose up, overflowed, and emptied into a sea of stories.

*

No matter how I tried to dismiss it, I harbored a suspicion that the results of my first HIV test had been wrong, that I'd been in the early stages of infection and hadn't developed antibodies. Besides, as long as I continued to have sex with Brian there was a chance, however slight, that I could become infected. And so one Christmas I decided to take the test again, having waited nearly two years rather than the recommended six months. I'd gotten used to my precarious sense of good health, and the first test had been traumatic enough to keep me away from doctors.

Though twice as expensive as a clinic, this time I chose an AIDS specialist whose practice was renowned for speedy lab work. My visit to his office, which had the brisk rhythm of an assembly line, ended when I wrote out a check and was given a number to phone after twelve noon three days later.

To my surprise, I didn't dwell on getting the results until a few hours before I made the call, when I paced in circles, checking the clock again and again. Time wound down, sluggish and grudging. Fear leaked into my fingers, my feet. By the time I dialed the telephone, my thoughts were hazy and disconnected.

"Last name?" asked the man on the other end. I envied his calm, his position of giving, rather than receiving, results. The silence that followed made me wonder if he'd put me on hold, if the office was unusually quiet, or if we'd been disconnected. Dull light streamed through the kitchen windows. The Hollywood Hills rose in the distance. Yellow smog varnished the sky. "Merry Christmas." His voice was cheerless, businesslike, so mismatched with what he said that I wasn't sure if I'd heard him correctly or even if he was the same man I'd been talking to a moment ago. "Merry Christmas," he said again. Had I dialed the right number? Maybe I'd accidentally called the gift-wrapping section of a department store.

"Am I OK?"

"Happy New Year."

"I am OK?"

"Have a good one."

"Oh," I said, remembering to breathe. "I get it."

A confidential test turned out to be part modern medicine, part espionage. The cryptic exchange had given me a sense of accomplishment, as if I'd learned a secret handshake or cracked a code. I phoned Brian immediately. I could hear the relief in his voice. Which made me love him. Which made me aware of the gulf between us. Which made me worry all over again. Which made me hate AIDS.

*

Six months ago, Brian experienced a bout of stomach cramps and diarrhea that was eventually diagnosed as cryptosporidium, a bacterium commonly found in drinking water. People with healthy immune systems are able to fight off the symptoms, while those with compromised immune systems cannot. This makes cryptosporidium an "AIDS-defining diagnosis." The actual illness, according to Brian, was fairly frightening, but not as frightening as it was to be put into this new category: a person with AIDS. Years' worth of fretful projections had done little to prepare us. For days afterward, every time we looked at each other the two of us burned with the need to speak, but we couldn't recall what we meant to say, couldn't dredge the words from our throats.

Eventually our shock and wordlessness wore off. And ever since it has, more and more clichés pertain — *I love you. I need you. We'll do what we have to.*

Given his stamina, it's often difficult to believe that Brian has AIDS. Most mornings he's been to the gym, eaten breakfast, and watered the plants by the time I awake. The garden blooms with towering aloe and orange hibiscus. He still works long hours at the office and sometimes seems more preoccupied with his clients' problems than with the virus thriving inside him. "What a day," he'll say, kicking off his shoes and switching on the TV. "You wouldn't believe the troubles I heard. We're really lucky." One night, the evening news tells of a celebrity dead of AIDS, and I ask Brian if hearing it frightens him. "I feel sad for them," he says, "not frightened for myself." He fights despair with tenacity and pursues new treatments. Coping with illness enhances rather than robs him of his virility. If his constant activity is, in part, an effort to avoid thinking about AIDS, his avoidance has a dynamic cast. Brian moves like a cubist figure, limbs cascading, tensions expressed.

At this point, we've been worn down by the likelihood of crisis even more than by crisis itself. We live in a state of continual vigilance. When the relentlessness of AIDS causes us to explode, it is usually over trivial things. Who should change a burned-out light bulb can escalate into a shouting match so fierce and loud and out of proportion, the two of us become red-faced, hoarse, indignant that one more thing can go wrong, that the world and all the objects in it will fail and break and leave us in the dark. At the heart of our argument lies a calm knowledge: this tantrum is impersonal, a vent through which frustration escapes.

Six years after Brian's HIV diagnosis, countless substances have been swallowed, injected, or absorbed through his skin: AZT, ddI, ddC, D4T, 3TC, Hydrea, Prednisone, Temovate, Sporanox, Septra, Dapsone, Trimethoprim, Zovirax, Mycobutin, Hydroxyzine, Diflucan, Decadrabulin, Zonalon, Humatin, Lomotil, Imodium, Hismanal, betamethasone, Nizoral, Lorazepam. He has to remember not only which medications to take, but when to take them, on an empty or a full stomach, making sure to watch out for allergic reactions, side effects, and photosensitivity. Blood tests, endoscopies, stool samples, X-rays — his health is like a second occupation.

"I'm sorry you have to go through this," I tell him.

"Let's hope," he says, "it only gets this bad."

It's possible that every one of his cells and organs has been saturated, altered forever by medication. And yet when I see or smell or touch him, my pang of recognition stays the same; he is still the man I know and want. Whether he is sick or well, I love the way he bears his body.

The moment before we make love, the future seems tethered to our lives by a long thread. It is difficult to believe what the disease is doing to him. Or what the disease is doing to him seems separate from who he is. Lined up on the table next to our bed are vials labeled "Morning," "Noon," and "Night," an experimental medication measured out like time itself. He is taking part in a "double-blind" study; some will be given the real drug, others a placebo. We whisk away the blanket. His hands are hot and dry and smooth. Double-blind, I think, as we close our eyes to kiss. I am no braver now than when our vigil began; what is at risk is greater than ever; I'm terrified of living without him, of dying alone. He draws me close, slips beneath me, his flesh the net that breaks my fall.

Tone Poem

〜〜〜〜〜〜〜〜〜

I wish I had one of those electronic keyboards where you can plug in prerecorded sounds that correspond to different keys. I'd compose an homage to insomnia — barking dogs and hammer blows and car alarms played over and over, the inverse of a lullaby, a score without a shred of respite. Try and get that tune out of your head. Or how about a nocturne for the aging body — the rumble of digestive juices, the suction of shoes that are pried from tired feet, the barely audible crackle of static as a brush is drawn through thinning hair. If only I'd had the foresight to tape-record every interesting snippet of conversation I've overheard in my long lifetime, by now I would have accumulated enough cryptic remarks, brilliant quips, and pretentious asides to pound out symphonic octaves of talk. I could pepper the punch line to my father's favorite joke — ". . . and the third nun says, 'Move over girls, I've got to gargle,'" — with scales of his helpless laughter. Here's an étude in which my absentminded mother keeps clearing her throat, and though she can't remember what she wanted to say, the ensuing silence is provocative, poignant, as sinewy and rich as a complex sentence.

Just to hear me practice any one of the tunes in my rapidly expanding repertoire would be like stomping through a minefield of burps, doorbells, cats in heat, and chattering teeth. It's late at night; melodies detonate inside my head; prongs are snug within the socket; the muse is She Who Must Have the Last Word. I crack my knuckles, take a breath. Let the neighbors beg me to shut my windows. Let them circulate petitions, file complaints. Let them leave at my doorstep, with anonymous notes, boxes of soundproof tile.

On the other hand, I wish I had an anechoic chamber, foam baffles padding the walls, in which to wile away the hours. I went inside one once at the Museum of Science and Industry, aware of a persistent hum I swore was coming from inside me. It was as if my restless, impressionable body had hoarded sounds since the day I was born, only to let loose with them in a room designed for absolute quiet. I felt phosphorescent with noise, like an amplified Fourth of July sparkler, sitting alone and emanating, or so it seemed, the rustle of my first blanket, the surf at Santa Monica beach, the ignition of every car I've driven. I don't know how many minutes I waited for blessed silence before I began to hear the forte chords of my own anatomy: the river of blood that ran through my ears, valves and sacs wheezing like bellows, a haunted house of creaking joints. "Help," I blurted, wanting out of my body as well as the room. But my voice was muffled by the spongy walls. It was like one of those nightmares in which you need to scream something in order to save your life, but not so much as a whimper comes out, your urgent words as dumb as rubber daggers.

After a mastoid operation, my mother took me to the doctor's office to have the bandage unwrapped. Dr. Holitzer worked solemnly, a concave mirror glinting on his forehead, his constant small talk meant to cheer a ten-year-old. Behind him hung a large chart showing a cross section of the human ear: the auditory canal, the hammer and anvil, the cochlea shaped like a seashell. "The improvement in your range of hearing," he said, "will take some getting used to." His voice boomed. His white coat crackled. The venetian blinds rattled like an avalanche of bones. He held a tuning fork up to my ear, and I remembered a B movie matinee: wincing Ulysses is strapped to the mast, the unbearably beautiful Siren song as piercing and shrill as a million kisses.

As a reward for my bravery, my mother walked me down Sixth Street to MacArthur Park, our footfalls loud and abrasive on the pavement. Paddleboats slapped the murky water. Pigeons grumbled under a shower of bread crumbs tossed by a grizzled indigent, as if motors chugged in their feathered chests. I was too old to hide beneath the dark wing of my mother's coat, but that's exactly what I wanted to do, incapable of conveying how rude and intrusive the city had become. Little man, my mother called me. But even her whispers were deafening, and I understood how kindness can hurt, can bruise the soft inner tissue.

It is thirty years later and my mother is dead, but her presence lingers like the peal of a bell. My father walks though the house they shared, feedback shrieking from his Miracle-Ear. Usually he pretends to hear me, nodding and smiling when I inquire how he is, an actor mugging in a silent movie. "Tuesday," he shouts when I ask him what he had for dinner. "Channel Two," he barks when I ask him if he's cold. Often, he forgoes the theatrics of understanding altogether, looking at me blankly, his head askew, as if I were speaking a foreign language, a language that it's far too late for him to learn. He takes the hearing aid out at night. The instant my father's head hits the pillow, he's oblivious to the telephone, fire trucks, pistol shots. On the still, unreachable island of his bed, he forgets the fury and bravura of the world.

Sometimes, at dawn, I burst through the seam between wakefulness and sleep like an acrobat through a paper hoop. There I am in my life again, eyes wide. I listen to birds fret in the trees, my bedroom walls ticking with warmth. The names of friends come back to me, things my parents said long ago, a tentative list of things to do, worries as stark and plaintive as prayers. Semiquavers, naturals, flats. Notes of a mounting crescendo.